*A New Birth of Freedom*

# A

# NEW BIRTH

# *of* FREEDOM

*Human Rights, Named and Unnamed*

CHARLES L. BLACK, JR.

YALE UNIVERSITY PRESS
NEW HAVEN AND LONDON

Book design by Debbie Glasserman.
Set in Weiss type.
Printed in the United States of America.

Library of Congress Cataloging-in-Publication Number 98-88790

ISBN 0-300-07734-3 (pbk.: alk.paper)

A catalogue record for this book is available from the British Library.

The paper in this book meets the guidelines for permanence and
durability of the Committee on Production Guidelines for Book
Longevity of the Council on Library Resources.

10   9   8   7   6   5   4   3   2   1

To the sacred memory of Abraham Lincoln

# Contents

FOREWORD BY PHILIP CHASE BOBBITT          ix

PREFACE          xix

Chapter 1    A GENERAL VIEW          1

Chapter 2    HUMAN RIGHTS AND THE STATES          41

Chapter 3    THE TRANSITIONAL FUNCTION OF
             "SUBSTANTIVE DUE PROCESS"          87

Chapter 4    JUDICIAL REVIEW AND MAJORITARIANISM          107

Chapter 5    THE CONSTITUTIONAL JUSTICE OF
             LIVELIHOOD          131

Chapter 6    OF TIME AND THE CONSTITUTION          141

             AN AFTERWORD          167

             NOTES          169

## Foreword

This book lays bare the legal foundation for those rights that, though not specifically named in the U.S. Constitution, cannot be dismissed if the deepest constitutional commitments of the American experiment are to be vindicated. That experiment took the European constitutional pattern of enumerated rights[1] and unenumerated powers[2] and turned it inside out. For the Americans, sovereignty itself was to be limited and the rights retained by the People were infinitely numbered. It was a source of grave concern to James Madison and Alexander Hamilton, the principal drafters of the *Federalist Papers*, that the movement to incorporate a Bill of Rights in the new U.S. Constitution would somehow becloud this radically new structure, with its list of specific powers and its implied domain of unassailable rights; if some rights were listed, they fretted, wouldn't there be a tendency to slight those rights that were not explicitly named? This problem was considerably deepened when, after the Civil War, the Constitution was amended to superimpose on the states the federal idea of limited powers and retained rights. Where were courts and other officials to look to determine the content and extent of these rights if they were never explicitly listed or described?

It is dramatically satisfying that the sword severing this Gordian knot should be wielded by Charles L. Black, Jr., now in his ninth decade. Charles Black was in his early forties when he wrote *The People and the Court* in 1960. This book was a frontal assault on the reigning dogma in elite constitutional circles whose biggest idea was that judicial review was fundamentally unsound. In this work Black endeavored to make judicial review respectable by giving it a *legal* rather than merely a *political* foundation. Thereafter he undertook much the same legitimizing task for the Supreme Court's action in *Brown v. Board of Education* in the most important article published by the *Yale Law Journal* in that decade, "The Lawfulness of the Segregation Decisions." Rereading this article now, with its mighty defense of arguments that, it must be said, are more to be inferred from than found in the *Brown* opinion, one can hardly imagine that there was a time when a different view of the Court's action widely prevailed. Most sound law professors and judges in the late fifties, however, would have thought Herbert Wechsler's 1959 "Neutral Principles" article to have said the last word on the subject: that there was simply no justification for preferring the rights of association of African Americans (who wished to integrate) to the same rights of those whites who wished to segregate themselves. Confronting this reluctant but principled stand, Black wrote, unforgettably, "Does segregation offend against equality?" After acknowledging that "[e]quality, like all general concepts, has marginal areas where philosophic difficulties are encountered," Black plainly and eloquently explains why he has no philosophic difficulty in concluding that segregation violates equality:

> [I]f a whole race of people finds itself confined within a system which is set up and continued for the very purpose of keeping it in an inferior station, and if the question is then solemnly propounded whether such a race is being treated "equally," I think we ought to exercise one of the sovereign prerogatives of philosophers—that of laughter. The only question remaining (after we get our laughter under control) is whether the segregation system answers to this description.
>
> Here, I must confess to a tendency to start laughing all over again. I was raised in the South, in a Texas city where the pattern of segregation was firmly fixed. I am sure it never occurred to anyone, white or colored, to question its meaning. The fiction of "equality" is just about on a level with the fiction of "finding" in the action of trover. [3]

In their concern with the primacy of doctrine, the law professors and, it must be added, some of the most prominent judges had simply neglected to appreciate that the system of legal segregation by color amounted to the setting up of a caste system by the State—an unquestionable violation of the State's relationship to its citizens, to say nothing of the plain words of the "equal protection" clause. The doctrine had become so severed from reality that plaintiffs and defendants, appellants and appellees had replaced flesh and blood human beings who were not symmetrically placed, like subatomic particles, but stood in historic situations unique to their time and situation.

Black was once described as "the only certified genius at the Yale Law School," and it is easy to see why. In addition to these pathbreaking constitutional works, he had coauthored with Grant Gilmore what remains the most important treatise on the law of Admiralty and published three books of highly praised poetry. I will not discuss these works as they are not directly germane to *New Birth of Freedom*, except to say that Black's inimitable prose style, which is in such fine evidence in these works, has also been important—I would even say necessary—in securing attention for his more radical constitutional ideas.

For the constitutional theorist Black's next work in 1969 was even more momentous than his earlier work: in *Structure and Relationship in Constitutional Law* Black definitively discredited the idea that the only legitimate constitutional arguments are derived from precedent or precedent itself derived from the history and text of the constitution. Just as influential in our constitutional development—as even a cursory reading of *McCulloch v. Maryland* would have indicated were it not for the blinders academic scholarship of this era had placed on lawyers and judges—were the structures set up by the constitution and the relationships among them that it mandated. This short work—only ninety-eight pages—has been so influential that now the words "history, structure and text" come as automatically to the tongue of the most chaste strict constructionist as "history and text" once did. Reflecting on this historic achievement, I wrote in

1987, "[I]f one looks across the scene of constitutional lawyers and judges of the present day, only Black can be ranked with the highest class [that would include Marshall and Story in the last century, and Brandeis, Holmes, and Hugo Black in this one.]"[4]

All comparisons are to some degree invidious; remarks like those just quoted are not calculated to endear one to one's contemporaries. Yet with each passing decade the essential truth of this paragraph seems more unassailable.

At present, Black's fame rests largely on his revitalization of the particular form of argument—structural argument—with which he is associated. Structural argument is one of half a dozen ways, or modalities, of framing legal arguments about the U.S. Constitution.[5] Although Black's name is most associated with structural argument, the present volume is, in some ways, a recognition of the limits of that form.

Structural argument reached its apogee in the early days of the Republic when its structures and relationships were first being hammered out, and then fell into disuse as other forms—chiefly doctrinal—achieved dominance. But in the turmoil following the *Brown* decision, doctrinal argument was not of much use; indeed *Plessy v. Ferguson* was a fifty-eight-year-old precedent when *Brown* effectively overruled it. Black reclaimed this form and, in his inimitable prose style, made it his own.

But there are limitations to any single form. Because structural argument derives its power from inferences arising from the political relationships ordained by the Constitution, it is of limited applicability to those human rights issues that are not, at bottom, about politics. It is a strain to suggest that the source of privacy rights lies in the freedom to assemble, or that *Roe v. Wade* is essentially a matter of federalism. While structural argument can provide useful insights into these questions, it misses something.

Rather it is in the realm of ethical argument that human rights questions must center. Like structural argument this form has been much neglected during most of this century in favor of sometimes highly attenuated doctrinal arguments. Thus it was felt that the justification of *Roe* had to be placed on *Griswold*—which provided a highly unconvincing basis—and cases like *Skinner* (involving a state program of eugenics) were absurdly tied to the vacuous, and therefore specious, jurisprudence of the equal protection amendment.

The difficulty with developing ethical argument is that it is usually confused with moral argument and thus with morality generally. The American moral ethos is simply not the same as its constitutional ethos; there is no warrant to read the moral preferences of judges—or anyone else—into the constitutional decisions of governments, no matter how pleasing this might sometimes be. Indeed the constitution is remarkably sparing in its moral preferences, choosing to leave most moral questions to the private sector. While there are many eloquent persons arguing that the Constitution enshrines their particular moral preferences, there is a profound difference between the legitimacy that moral debate confers and that offered by legal argument.

Indeed, much is sacrificed by trying to make moral and legal argument coextensive. Although there is a wide spectrum of opinion on the proper role of marriage, for example, there is a general consensus that the State cannot dictate whom we marry; while there is an active debate on whether or not couples should employ artificial means of birth control, there is a similar consensus that the State cannot simply forbid contraception; and so on with respect to procreation and the right to educate one's children and determine one's own medical care. The difficulty is that when the Supreme Court has recognized these intuitively obvious rights, there has been precious little in the way of constitutional text or original intent or political structure to which the Court could turn. The rights that we can infer from the most basic American constitutional ideas of limited sovereignty and the enumeration of powers are, after all, themselves unenumerated. Perhaps for this reason, the doctrine which has been purpose built to support these holdings—"substantive" due process—has never been able quite to shed its factitious aura and as a result has been an easy target for every critic whose ultimate argument is "Oh yeah? Where does it say that?"[6]

Charles Black, in the book that follows, has taken up the task of providing a constitutional basis for decisions that construe the unenumerated rights of the Constitution. The same man who provided legal arguments for *Brown* when these were sorely needed has now accomplished the same task with respect to *Meyer*, *Pierce*, *Griswold*, and *Skinner*. In this book, the reader will once again find the watermarks of Black's work: the powerful, lucid prose, the careful, pivotal observation, and above all, the craftsman's art of legal argument. In his own words, Black seeks "the construction of a better system of reason" for the constitutional law of the unenumerated rights.

Here, as before, Black is, at bottom, concerned with legitimacy and with providing for lawyers and judges and other public officials the means of reaching satisfying conclusions that comport with the country's deepest sense of its constitutional self.

It is a widespread misperception among the laity that law is an edifice of incomprehensible complexity and that its most magnificent chambers are reserved for those who not only tolerate but seek the counterintuitive, arcane, and contradictory. Every now and then the public reacts to this misunderstanding by demanding that law be "simplified." The great codification movements of the last part of the nineteenth century were one such reaction.

In truth, the surest expressions of law are the clearest. It is not necessary to "simplify" or to distort the law in order to bring it into line with our deepest convictions of common sense. What is required is careful and conscientious adherence to what Charles Black has called "the manner of legal reasoning." Those who have sought to assist the movement toward the recognition of human rights by abandoning close adherence to the modalities of constitutional argument have therefore done this cause no positive service.

Rather, the ones to whom we are most indebted are those who have dived down the deepest to our sense of fitness and stayed down long enough to craft distinctly legal arguments that serve that sense. Charles Black's work is not powerful because it is beautiful, having been rendered by a poet; rather it is beautiful because it is powerful—because, that is, it is the product of the arts of law, and thus is linked to our sense of rightness.

On the wall of my office at the University of Texas is a large, framed excerpt from Charles Black's "The Two Cities of Law," handwritten by him for my graduation from Law School in 1975. It is evidence of Black's long preoccupation with the subject he has taken up in the present book:

> One afternoon last fall I was on my way to my class in Constitutional Law. I was going to lead a discussion of certain technicalities having to do with the application of the Fourteenth Amendment, as implemented by acts of Congress, to voting and other rights. My head was full of section numbers in The Federal Revised Statutes. I fear I was mumbling to myself, a practice I cannot recommend to those who hold reputation dear.
>
> I happen to look up—all the way up, over the tops of the red stone buildings into the sky as the Indians of Connecticut must have seen it before the white settlers came, with the great autumnal castles of clouds as far as the imagination could reach. And somehow, very suddenly, all this illimitable expansiveness and lofty freedom connected within me the words I was tracing from the Fourteenth Amendment though the statute books— "privileges or immunities of citizens," "due process of law," "equal protection of the laws." And I was caught for a moment by the feeling of a Commonwealth in which these words had not the narrow, culture-bound relative meaning we are able to give them in the "real" world, but were grown to the vastness that is germinal within them.

This sense of the transcendent is finely fitted with Black's superb and careful craftsmanship. Perhaps neither trait alone would have marked him as the most gifted of constitutional exponents. Together they have assured his stature as the most profound. The marvelous promise of his early work—like the epic promises he writes about in this book— have been richly fulfilled in Black's contribution to the jurisprudence of the American constitution.

—Philip Chase Bobbitt

## Preface

This book puts forward the thesis that a sound and satisfying foundation for a general and fully national American law of human rights exists in three imperishable commitments—the Declaration of Independence, the Ninth Amendment, and the "citizenship" and "privileges and immunities" clauses of Section 1 of the Fourteenth Amendment (as those clauses ought to have been and still ought to be interpreted). These three commitments speak in solemn organic harmony. They ought at long last to be attended to as they stand—for as they stand, in their harmony, they are all we have and all we need of prime authority for our building, by the methods of law, a never-to-be-finished edifice of human rights.

I write out of fifty years' professional thought and work and feeling on and around these things. There is an enormous and many-sided literature—from that half-century and from long before. I have been concerned in this short book to state and to support, in my own voice, my own life's conclusions. I have drawn freely from my earlier writings, improving them when I can. But I think this book has its own new unity.

I know that my chief debt, far outweighing all others, is to Abraham Lincoln; once one takes courage from his recognition of the primacy of the Declaration of Independence, the rest falls easily into place.

I have been heartened through the years by the work of Kenneth Karst on the fruitfulness of the promise in "citizenship": he and I have cultivated bordering acres of this field.

I owe thanks to Jack Greenberg, Philip Bobbitt, and Walter Dellinger, for decades of exchange of ideas with them— and, more than that, for their friendship.

And to Jane Isay, now as in the past, my Editor-in-Chief.

And to Barbara Aronstein Black (if I may be indulged in one more repetition of a thought never absent from my heart) for everything.

—C.L.B., Jr.
Columbia Law School
February 1997

*A New Birth of Freedom*

## Chapter 1

# A

# GENERAL

# VIEW

This work is being undertaken to set upon a firmer and wider ground of legitimacy the human-rights law of the United States. In performing such a task, one always encounters new insights suggested in part by one's earlier works[1] and by their mutual harmonies.

Something else is perhaps not too obvious to mention. For a man of full four-score winters, to whom promotion through publication is no longer a possibility or even a good, to sit down of his own free will and write yet another book—for him to take that much time away from playing with his grandchildren—he must think he has something that needs to be said:

*The foundations of American human-rights law are in bad shape. They creak, they groan for rebuilding.*

Ours is a nation that founded its very right to exist on the ground of its commitment to the securing of nobly envisioned human rights in very wide comprehension—a country that now bases its claim to the world's regard on a questing devotion to the securing of human rights. When we are true to ourselves, to our own beginnings and to the best of our history, we do not assert our entitlement to something called "world leadership" on the ground of our now being "the only superpower"—that is, after all, just the bully's reason for claiming dominance—but on our commitment to human rights.

This first chapter will present the outline of the fresh foundation—built of venerable materials—that I propose to defend in this book. But I believe it wise to start with a preliminary overview of the principal lacks, as I see them, of the present human-rights law of the United States.

First, the "enumerated" (or textually specified) rights found in the Constitution and in our Bill of Rights—the first eight amendments—are very plainly insufficient to found a system broad and comprehensive enough for a really free people to walk around in. The validation of this statement calls for the reading of a few hundred words. I will take you through that reading later. (Maybe someday we'll compose a "round robin" to the people at Philip Morris Company, who have so reverentially eulogized the Bill of Rights as the "onlie begetter" of our ensuing liberties.)

Secondly, the guarantees of the post–Civil War constitutional amendments, as the Supreme Court has read them, have not come near to filling this deficiency. The Fourteenth Amendment guarantee of "due process of law" can and to a large extent does combine with the same clause in the Fifth Amendment to ground a developing series of national rights to "fair *procedure.*" But this does not, on its face or in the normal meaning of its words, or in its natural implications, guarantee any *substantive* human rights. It says, for example, that you cannot be tried before a bribed judge, or without being informed of the charge against you. But it does not say that

you cannot be sent to prison by an unbribed tribunal for marrying before the age of forty, if a state statute sets that as the
minimum age—provided only that the trial, by which you are
found guilty in fact of marrying at thirty-nine, is *procedurally*
fair.

Thirdly (as a desperate answer to a desperate need), a thing
called "substantive due process" has been thought up (I had
almost written "dreamed up") as a ground for the protection
of substantive rights, such as the right to marry, to have or not
to have children, to send those children to religious or military school, to teach and learn German, to listen to rock
music, to travel from one State to another, not to have your
property taken by a State without compensation. This paradoxical, even oxymoronic phrase—*"substantive* due *process"*—
has been inflated into a patched and leaky tire on which
precariously rides the load of some substantive human rights
not named in the Constitution.

Its application follows no sound methods of interpretation
(how could it, given the nature of the phrase itself?) and is
therefore neither reliably invocable in cases that come up, nor
forecastable in result by anything much but a guess. This kind
of non-standard is not good enough for a systematic equity
of human rights. It everlastingly will not do; it is *infra dignitatem*, it leaks in the front and leaks in the back. The anxiety
it produces (especially in judges—see below pp. 105–106) is
an ill-tuned, wavering keynote for a system of human-rights
law.

Fourthly, the most comprehensive and promising words in
the post–Civil War amendments—the "citizenship" and "privileges and immunities" clauses of the Fourteenth Amendment—have been put into suspended animation by a

not-very-clever conjurer's trick, maladroit at best, though more serious charges than that of mere incompetence may apply (see below pp. 55–85).

Fifthly, the "equal protection" clause of the Fourteenth Amendment is of force, on its face, only against the States. Its application against the national government has to wriggle like a rabbit pulled by its ears out of a hat.

Sixthly, the guarantees embodied in the First Amendment are not stated as applying against the States and their subdivisions. He who runs may read: "*Congress* shall make no law . . ."

Now that's quite a list. It comprises only highlights. We ought not to be content to face the twenty-first century with a patchy, tacky human-rights law, so poorly legitimated, so feeble of reason.

I could expand greatly on each of these statements, and will do so further on. You can't afford to rely on my mere assertion. But at least you now can see how this octogenarian, having long considered all these defects, thinks it worthwhile to take some time away from the grandchildren to write this book. Indeed, you'll discern that writing this book is not really taking time from the grandchildren; it is being written for the sake of all our grandchildren—in whose number I naturally, even with a certain special pride, include my own. This book attempts the construction of a *better system of reason* for the grounding of constitutional human rights in this country.

We Americans first entered and still hold ourselves out on the stage of the world as a people and as a power dedicated to the

securing of human rights; we were the very first people formally to make that seminal commitment. That is the way we
have been thought of on Wenceslaus and Tienanmen Squares.
Even more important, that is the way we want and need to
think about ourselves.

We are also a people, and want to be looked on as a people, dedicated to the rule of law. It was, then, inevitable that
we should use law for the delineation and the sustaining of
human rights.

Given these two things, it came to us naturally to be the
people, of all the peoples of the world, who some two hundred years ago invented the idea that the very *Constitution* of
a country—the document, that is to say, that *constitutes*, that
establishes, empowers and shapes the structures of government, and that declares itself to be the "supreme Law of the
Land"—should set up, in the same breath of history, and with
the same authority, certain affirmative guarantees of human
rights under law.

Law is reasoning from commitment. Where do we find those
commitments from which we may derive our reasoned constitutional law of human rights?

On the highest level and of fully general scope, there are
just three such commitments: (1) the opening paragraphs of
the Declaration of Independence (1776); (2) the Ninth
Amendment to our Constitution (1791); and (3) the thirty
words or so that are the "citizenship" and "privileges and immunities" clauses of Section 1 of the Fourteenth Amendment
(1868) thereto.

That is all we have of first-water, unassailably authoritative commitment to substantive human rights in general. It is the keystone thesis of this book that these three utterances, unmatchable as they are in authority, constitute (each severally and the three in harmony) all the commitment we need from which to reason—*after the manner of law's reasoning*[2]—to an open-ended and open-textured series of human rights.

All we have, and all we need? It's worth taking another look at them.

First, the Declaration of Independence. That rather short document was not a Fourth of July oration (the first one of those was doubtless delivered on 4 July 1777) but a distinctly juristic act—the foundation of all later juristic acts in our territory. Near its beginning it declares, as foundation for all its claims:

> "We hold these truth to be self-evident, that all Men are created equal, that they are endowed by their Creator with certain inalienable Rights, that among these are life, liberty, and the Pursuit of Happiness—that to secure these rights, Governments are instituted among men. . . ."

It was no less a man than Calvin Coolidge who said, "The business of America is business." I have always found this utterance repellently close to the even terser "Business is business," which is what you say when you propose to deal with somebody for your own gain alone, without alloy of humaneness, generosity, or charity. But Silent Cal was a century and a half late in defining the "business" of America. The Declaration of Independence did that, and will continue to do so until we decide formally to repudiate it. To paraphrase Dr. Johnson, the cultivation of human rights is the invaluable part of the business of our nation.

Should the Declaration be taken seriously? Well, the people who uttered this document pledged to its support their lives, their fortunes, and their sacred honor. That does sound a bit like a Fourth of July oration, doesn't it? But think again before you commit to that judgment. All the people who signed did so with the knowledge that they were taking a substantial chance of incurring the penalties of treason—hanging, drawing and quartering, forfeiture by attainder of all their property, and being branded with the hateful name "traitor." Some of them may have thought, or hoped, that the British government would not proceed to those extremes. But who, in the early days of a war, knows how bitter the events of that war, and the feelings engendered by those events, may become? These people were knowingly and literally endangering their lives, their fortunes, and their sacred honor. Can we think it right—in a time when the word "superpower" applies to us alone (Acton, thou shouldst be living at this hour!), while Britain is a mellowed old friend—to treat as mere bombast the words these people used formally to justify their great action to the world? How frivolous dare we be with our original and irreplaceable commitment?

When we consider the Declaration as a commitment of the new nation to a general system of human rights, to the "securing" of such rights as the ground for the very legitimacy of the nation, it is the short passage just quoted that must interest us. Since the organic connection of this passage with later commitments (the Ninth Amendment and the "citizenship" and "privileges and immunities" clauses of the Fourteenth Amendment) is the unifying concern of this whole book, I shall leave the matter at that, touching for now on only one collateral question about the Declaration. Since we are examining the commitment of this nation to a *law* of human rights, we must here consider the force, *in law*, of the doctrines of the Declaration of Independence.

It is my own view that the doctrines of the Declaration should be taken to have the force of *law*—the force *in law* of general commitments from which *particular* law can be derived. For a reason which will very soon appear, it is not necessary to insist upon this. But I will briefly give my grounds, because (whether my view be fully accepted or not) the rehearsal of these grounds, slightly transposed, can make clear the appropriateness of the Declaration as a *basis* for law, as a *nourisher* of law, whether or not it be taken to be law of its own unaided force.

The Declaration as a whole was an act of "constitution," a *juristic* act, an act of *law*, after the manner of law in all its fields, quite as surely as is a statute setting up a state police force. The operative passage is the penultimate sentence:

> We, therefore, the Representatives of the United States of America, in General Congress, Assembled, appealing to the Supreme Judge of the world for the rectitude of our intentions, do, in the Name, and by Authority of the good People of these Colonies, solemnly publish and declare, That these United Colonies are, and of Right ought to be Free and Independent States; that they are Absolved from all Allegiance to the British Crown, and that all political connection between them and the State of Great Britain, is and ought to be totally dissolved; and that as Free and Independent States, they have full Power to levy War, conclude Peace, contract Alliances, establish Commerce, and to do all other Acts and Things which Independent States may of right do.

These words demolish one legal authority and set up another. They are, then, *constitutive* words, constitutive of the authority of the United States, as that authority has been transmitted and developed down to now. The Declaration is the root of all political authority among us, of all legitimate exercise of power.

The Declaration (a short document) gives its reason for this new constitution of the basis of law, and the reason the signers consider themselves authorized to make such a change, in its second paragraph. That reason was that the British power had crossed the bounds *of legitimacy*, in that it had offended against the rights named in the second paragraph of the Declaration ("life, liberty, and the pursuit of happiness") and had thus failed in its radical and indispensable duty, as a "government"—the duty to "secure" these rights.

It is hard for me to believe that a political organism that places its right to life on these clearly expressed grounds can walk away from the legal obligation based on this constitutive fact of its history. The scope of such an obligation is bounded by prudent possibility, and we ought not be too hard on those who wobbled and trembled in the awful shadow of slavery. Let the dead past bury its pitiful dead— but we ought not to leave that past buried in darkness. Nor the obligations created by past acts at the beginning of our life. If we do that, what right do we have to spout the Declaration's words on the "Voice of America"? It may be too late to mend with full efficacy, but it's never too late to mend.

Should chattel slavery, now 130 years gone, continue to cast a killing shadow on our noblest and most fundamental utterance, as it continues to cast a cold shadow on the lives and hopes of black people?

Now you may not be convinced that the Declaration should be looked on as having permanent standing as a source of law. After all, this constitutive, supra-constitutional act, grounding all our later political acts, and in its expressive force binding all "governments"—national, state, county, city, drainage districts—doesn't *say* that it is "law." So let us pass on to the Ninth Amendment to our Constitution.

The Constitution of the United States—of which the Ninth Amendment is "to all Intents and Purposes" a part (Article V)—*does* declare itself to be law, part of "the supreme Law of the Land" (Article VI).

In 1791, less than fifteen years after the signing of the Declaration of Independence, this Ninth Amendment to the Constitution came into effect, having been drafted and submitted by the First Congress in 1789, thirteen years after the Declaration of Independence. The Ninth Amendment, pursuant to Article V of the Constitution, then became "valid *to all Intents and Purposes* as part of this Constitution" and therefore a coequal working part of "the supreme Law of the Land."

The Ninth Amendment provides: "The enumeration in the Constitution, of certain rights, shall not be construed to deny or disparage others retained by the people."

The academic writing on this Amendment seems to me to be in great part a multidirectional fluttering flight from the Amendment's rather plain meaning, a flight set going by the fact that the Ninth Amendment seems to be repudiating decisively the idea that no constitutional human right can be valid unless it is enumerated—or named—in the Constitution.

I can't make a better start here than by setting down my own earlier thoughts on this, with some slight clerical changes.[3]

This sentence stands at the end of a very short "enumeration" of rights—an "enumeration" nobody could possibly think anywhere near sufficient for guarding even the values it patchily and partially shields. The Ninth Amendment language was put where it is by people who believed they were enacting for an indefinite future. All sorts of other language may have been used around this language. But this was the language chosen to become "valid to all Intents and Purposes, as Part of [the] Constitution. . . ." What does it seem to be saying?

It could be read as saying that nobody really ought to deny, in discourse of a mixed moral and political tenor, that a number of rights exist, beyond the "enumerated" ones. But this is quite unbelievable. Virtually all of the Constitution, including the amendments preceding and later following this one, is *law*, sparely stated in the language of law. Attention here should be focused especially on the first eight amendments, together with which the Ninth Amendment entered the Constitution. These are austere, peremptory directions to lawmaking and law-enforcing officials, from Congress, through courts of law, down to magistrates issuing search warrants and military officers quartering troops. In the Constitution as a whole, and in this immediate context, the insertion of a precept of moral philosophy would not merely have changed the subject abruptly, but would have put the content of this Amendment in quite a different world than that of the Constitution, and of the "enumerated" rights just set out.

The Amendment could be read as saying no more than that

the bare fact of "enumeration" of other rights should not, in and of itself, give rise to the inference that no other rights exist, but that the forbidding of the drawing of this one inference in no way prejudices the question whether there really are, in addition to the enumerated rights, any "others retained by the people." I guess a computer, fed the words, would have to print this out as a logical possibility. I submit that it is not a serious psychological possibility that anyone quite neutral on the question of the existence of rights not "enumerated" would bother to set up this kind of directive as to what course the non-logic of *expressio unius* may take, leaving it quite open that the very same conclusion—no non-enumerated rights—may be reached by some other path of reasoning. The Ninth Amendment seems to be guarding something; such bother is not likely to be taken if the question is thought to be quite at large whether there is anything out there to be guarded.

It should be noted, in passing, that the most one could get out of even this computer printout is that the language of the Ninth Amendment does not *affirmatively imply* the existence of unenumerated rights; even a computer would have to print out that this language implies that such rights *may* exist—if you also fed into that computer the assumption, "The utterers of this language were not talking just to hear their heads rattle." This, while not strictly an existence-proof, would be a proof of the serious possibility of the existence of rights not enumerated; even this might be enough to legitimate a further quest. But the Constitution is not a computer program, and I submit that the preponderance of reason leaves us with the conclusion, about as well-supported as any we can reach in law, that the Ninth Amendment declares as a matter of law—of constitutional law, overriding other law—that some other rights are "retained by the people," and that these shall be treated as *on an equal footing* with rights enumerated.

This would have to mean that these rights "not enumerated" may serve as the substantive basis for judicial review of governmental actions; any other conclusion would not only do violence to expectations naturally shaped by the command that these other rights not be "denied or disparaged" in respect to the enumerated rights, but would also lead one back around to the inadmissible theory, discussed above, that this Amendment, placed where it is, is merely a directive for the course of moral philosophy or of purely political argument. Nor does it make any difference whether the possibility of judicial review was immediately present to everyone's mind at just the moment the Ninth Amendment passed Congress, or was ratified by the last necessary State. The idea that constitutional rights were to form the substantive basis of such review was so much in the air (and in the laws[4]) that it is unlikely that it was overlooked. But in any case the direction of the Ninth Amendment—that nonenumerated rights not be "denied or disparaged," as against enumerated rights—was directed literally at the future, at the corpus of law-to-be, and affirmative settlement of the question (if, as I more than doubt, it was a real question in 1790) of the rightness of judicial review, on the basis of *any* right "enumerated" in the Constitution, would settle the rightness of judicial review on the basis of those rights not enumerated, though "retained by the people," because anything else would "deny or disparage" these latter, in a quite efficacious way.

The only hitch is, in short, that the rights not enumerated are not enumerated. We are not told what they are. So the question is, "What do you do when you are solemnly told, by an authority to which you owe fidelity, to protect a generally designated set of things in a certain way, but are, in the very nature of the case, not told what particular things this set comprises?"

These are two possible courses to follow. One is to throw up your hands and say that no action is possible, because you haven't been told exactly how to act. The other is to take the Ninth Amendment as a command to use any rational methods available to the art of law, and with these in hand to set out to discover what it is you are to protect.

The first of these leads right back around, yet again, to a *practical* "denial and disparagement" of the rights not enumerated; it leads, indeed, to something a shade more imbecile than taking the Amendment as a direction of the course of moral philosophy, for it disclaims any power even to discover what rights are not to be "denied or disparaged" in out-of-court discourse. But at least you stay out of trouble.

The second course gets you into deep troubles. First is the trouble of deciding, by preponderance of reason, what methods are to be seen as legitimate, in our legal culture, for making out the shape of rights not named. Then there is the trouble—since no known legal method produces anything like certain results—of deciding where the preponderance of reason lies on the merits of *any particular claim of right*, when that claim is weighed by the methods you decide are legitimate. And the worst of it is that these troubles will never be done with, or even lessened. The methods of law are not a closed

canon. The problems they must solve are infinite and unforeseeable. The solutions will never have the quality of the
Pythagorean Theorem; time may even bring the conviction
that some solutions, though confidently arrived at, were
wrong, and must be revised.

Altogether, it's a pack of troubles. Maybe we ought to give
up, and let the Ninth Amendment—and the priceless rights
it refers to—keep gathering dust for a third century.

But there is one thing to note about the very real troubles
that face us when we turn to the search that the Ninth Amendment seems to command. *These are the troubles not of the Ninth
Amendment alone, but of law itself.* If they put one off the Ninth
Amendment enterprise, maybe one ought to give up law altogether, try something else. But that course has its own problems. To turn to medicine, to music, to history—even to
mathematical physics—is to accept the burden of troubles
somewhat resembling those of Ninth Amendment law, or of
law as a whole. For my part, too far superannuated to train for
anything else, I would accept the challenge of Ninth Amendment law, as the same old (and forever new) challenge of law.

What methods are legitimate for finding and giving shape
to the nonenumerated rights guarded by the Ninth Amendment?

Let me start with a rejection. Some people, faced with this
question, would try to dig up every scrap of paper that happens to have survived since the eighteenth century; and to
piece together some sort of "intent,"[5] with very little weight
given to the transcendently relevant piece of paper, the one
on which the duly enacted text of the Ninth Amendment was
written.

I am one who thinks that, in a general way, our legal culture carries this sort of thing much too far. We sometimes treat statements made informally in one House of Congress as the exact equivalent, in everything but name, of formal statutory language; if it is right to do that, what are the formalities for? In the very teeth of Madison's quite sound and reiterated insistence that the confidential records of the 1787 Convention, not being publicly known until decades after the government was formed, ought not to be used to establish the public meaning of the Constitution's text, we sometimes seem to treat these records as all but superior in authority to that text itself. If we had to choose between our style of getting drunk on collateral and sometimes casual evidences of "intent," and leaving the stuff altogether alone, as the British did for centuries, I would choose the latter course—though I think sometimes a very cautious use of such material may be warranted.

But if there ever was a case where informal collateral evidence of "intent" must be useless, it is in regard to the finding of the rights that belong in the class of "others retained by the people." This language of the Ninth Amendment is apt for referring to things you haven't thought of or quite agreed upon; such language would be hopelessly inapt as a sort of coded-message reference to a closed class of "rights" you *have* thought of and agreed upon. If the decoded message read that rights A, B, C, D, *and no others,* were not to be "denied or disparaged," then the peculiar result would have been reached that we would have two kinds of "enumeration," the second kind being a coded enumeration, and that these *two* kinds of "enumeration" exhausted the class of rights to be protected, so that other rights, not thus "enumerated," *could* be "denied or disparaged." The informally arrived-at "enumeration" would thus be given an *expressio unius* force explicitly denied to the formal "enumeration" elsewhere. Something would have gone wrong here; doubtless the Greeks had a word for that kind of paradox. I am content to say that it seems to me to have no place in the robust common-sense world of the best work on American constitutional law.

Some pause might be given if we found a real consensus, uniting the *major pars* of the relevant eighteenth-century people, that some identifiable claim to a "right" was not to be looked on as guarded by the Ninth Amendment. But this would be a pause only. "Due process" is an evolving concept; "cruel and unusual punishment" is an evolving concept; the language of the Ninth Amendment seems even more apt than these to be mentioning an evolving set of rights, not to be bounded even by a negative eighteenth-century judgment based on eighteenth-century evaluations, and social facts as then seen.

I have treated this issue of collaterally evidenced "intent" quite abstractly; I don't know of any corpus of actual evidence that would enable or oblige one to treat it more concretely.

To me, the upshot is that we have to take this language as it comes to us. We are its inheritors; it "belongs in usufruct to the living," as Jefferson said of the earth. If we regard it (as I do) as directing us to do our best to discover for ourselves what unenumerated rights are to be given sanction, so that we may obey the Ninth Amendment command against their denial or disparagement, there is really no dearth of sound and well-tested methods for obeying this command, and so for moving in the direction of a rational and coherent *corpus juris* of human rights.

This statement gains a great deal of plausibility, or more, from the fact that that we have for a very long time been protecting unnamed (that is to say, "unenumerated") rights. We have done this, sometimes, under the guise of treating the language of the Constitution as highly metaphoric or otherwise figurative, as when we see "speech" in black armbands,[6] or see the making of a continuously disturbing noise near someone's land as a "taking."[7] But the *appropriateness* of any such metaphoric extension can be explored only by asking, for example, "Is the wearing of a black armband in the context in which we encounter it so similar, *in relevant respects*, to speech, that it ought to be treated as speech is treated?" And when we ask this question we recognize an old friend—the common-law method of arguing from the established to the not yet established, weighing similarities and differences, and deciding where the balance lies. Sometimes, as in the common law, this method creates a whole new heading, as with the "freedom of association" now generally recognized as arising, by the discernment of analogy, with the First Amendment rights literally "enumerated."[8] That is how we achieved the result of applying the double-jeopardy clause to cases where *imprisonment* or a fine is the penalty, though, if you read the Fifth Amendment, you find that, as named or "enumerated," this protection applies only to "jeopardy of life or limb." If, in time of peace, government attempted the "quartering" of sailors or government civilian employees in houses without the consent of the owners, or if consent was had from the "owner" of an apartment house but not from a tenant in possession under a lease, rational legal discourse could be addressed to the questions all these actions would raise in confrontation with the Third Amendment. You could, of course, talk as though the questions were whether a sailor is "really" a soldier, whether the tenant of an apartment is "really" the part-owner of a "house"—but even in this disguise these questions could be rationally addressed only by adding to them the phrase "in preponderantly relevant respects," or some such language. And this would lead right into the eternal question, "Is this a difference that *ought to make a difference?*" This question sounds familiar, because it is, first, a question repeated infinite times in the quest for rational justice, and, secondly, because it is the question continually asked—and answered in each case as best it may be—by the common law, the matrix of all our particular legal methodology. The issue is not whether the use of this method would be a bizarre innovation; the issue is whether any quest for decent law, with its parts rationally related, can possibly do without it.

Nor need this method of "analogy" be used only for small motions, like the supplying of the hiatus in the double jeopardy clause. The seeking of consistent rationality is a requirement of all good law, at every level of generality. If the central meaning of the equal protection clause is—as it pretty surely is—the forbidding of discrimination against *blacks*, then the propriety of applying that clause to discrimination against *women* can be reasoned about by marshaling the similarities (the genetic character of the trait, the maintenance of a grievously discriminatory regime by social stereotypes, and so on) in confrontation with the differences (for example, absence of whole-family discrimination stretching back through history). And since this is both a real and a complicated case, the Nineteenth Amendment would also serve as a starting-point for the eternal similarity-difference reasoning of law questing for justice: If women may not be excluded from voting, may they be excluded from office-holding? From jury service? And so on.

I must resist the impulse toward—and am really glad to eschew—any attempt here and now, or ever, to build a *corpus juris* of human rights on this basis, or on the others to be mentioned below. In a proper and profound sense, that corpus will never be built; it will always be building, like the common law at its best. If this method is not rational, then neither is the common law. And neither is any other attempt to give due effect to similarities and differences between already decided and newly presented cases and problems.

There is another generative principle in our legal system, the principle that law may be generated by due attention to the sound requirements arising out of social or political structures and relations.[9] This is how we got the warranty of fitness for human consumption in the sale of food; this is also how, in some States, we have recently gotten that warranty extended to bind the manufacturer and packager or canner, when structures and relationships changed in the food trade. This is how we got the insurers' right of subrogation, and the testimonial privilege for communications between penitent and priest. This is how we got the obligation of parents to care for their children. Our law—and, I venture to say, *all* law—has been and is continuously being shaped and reshaped by this generative principle. It is the principle from which we first derived the right, not literally "enumerated," to move from one State to another—a right established without reliance on any text.[10]

Now if we had only these two master methods—the method of similarity-difference reasoning from the committed to the not yet committed, and the method of reasoning from structures and relationships—we would have the means of building toward a rationally consistent, comprehensive, and fairly serviceable law of human rights. There is no question here of discerning that these rights are in any designative sense "mentioned" or "incorporated" in the Ninth Amendment, or that they derive from that Amendment; the language of the Amendment suggests—or commands, as I think—a quest outside itself, a quest for rights *nowhere* enumerated, not the mere tracing out of its references, which are, in the very nature of the case, of total vagueness.

*structural-ism*

But methods, in any mature and subtle legal culture, are never a closed class. Law ought to be seen to contain not only the means of striving toward rational consistency, not only the means of keeping the rules of legal decision in tune with the society's structures and relationships, but also the means—the methods—for reaching toward higher goals. Herein is the very best of what was so beautifully called, by Lon Fuller, "The Law in Quest of Itself." With the carefulness that is a condition of law's rationality, we may be able to discern and validate "other [rights] retained by the people" as latent in, and therefore susceptible of being drawn from, the noblest of concepts to which our nation is committed.

*education*

The earliest and best-attested source for such concepts is the Declaration of Independence. There is, then, a shorter way toward giving abundant application to the Ninth Amendment.

The Amendment speaks of rights *"retained* by the people,"— "retained," that is to say, in 1789—enacting that these are not to be "denied or disparaged" by virtue of their not having been "enumerated in the Constitution." The crucial word is "retained." What "rights" could "the people" be thought to have had *before* the enactment of this Amendment, though these are not "enumerated" in the Constitution?

Well, as we have seen, just thirteen years (a little more than two Reagan terms and one Bush term) before the Ninth Amendment went out to the States, the Declaration of Independence said that all mankind had certain rights—stated with great generality and with the greatest possible emphasis. Were these 1776 rights "retained by the people" in 1789? In 1791? They were said to be "inalienable." When and how were they "alienated" in that brief interval?

We are not talking about a time interval like the 450 years between Magna Carta and the coronation of William and Mary, wherein words may have undergone deep semantic metamorphoses. Let's make this a little more concrete. Of the fifty-five signers of the Declaration of Independence, thirty-four were still living when the Ninth Amendment became law. Some of them lived ten years longer; a few even longer than that. The Declaration of Independence and the Ninth Amendment are virtually contemporaneous documents. Their verbal fit is close: "All men" = "the people." The word "rights" is the key word in both. The word "retained," in the Ninth Amendment, exactly fits the situation, if you so much as take the Declaration at all seriously.

Thirteen years is a mighty short time for the vanishing of inalienable rights given by God—an attribution surely intimating some feel of permanency, even if you think that God is just a ghost story.

Let me move on to complete the tripartite canon. (It is well to put these things in place together and at the start; we will be continually returning to them throughout the book.)

After our great Civil War, several Amendments to the Constitution were put in effect. (I remind you that the putting into effect of an Amendment to the Constitution is the most formal and authoritative act of which the American people are capable.) Slavery was abolished in 1865 (Amendment XIII) and in 1870 racial discrimination in voting eligibility was forbidden (Amendment XV). All who know the realistic history of Negro voting in the ninety-five years following this latter Amendment, in a large section of the country (a history graced by such monkey-tricks as the "white primary"), will smile. But the principle had been committed to in a form which could not be defaced by long years, and which at last shows signs of coming into and holding its own.

Between these two Amendments, in 1868, the Fourteenth Amendment came into the Constitution. It is a complicated thing, but we do not for our purposes need to go through it all. It will be enough to quote its first lines, the last words in our precious three-part charter of substantive human rights: "Section 1. All persons born or naturalized in the United States, and subject to the jurisdiction thereof, are citizens of the United States and of the State wherein they reside. No State shall make or enforce any law which shall abridge the privileges or immunities of citizens of the United States . . ."

It should be noted carefully that, under this provision, not only *national* citizenship but also *state* citizenship is conferred

on certain vast classes of persons as a matter of *national* constitutional law. If you are born in the United States or are naturalized in the United States, then you are a citizen of the
United States. If, being such a citizen of the United States,
you live in Texas, then the *national* law of this Amendment or-
dains that you are a citizen of Texas; Texas has nothing to say
about the matter. Not 10%, not 1%, just nothing. If you leave
Texas and set up a residence in California instead, then you
are, under the edict of *national* law, a citizen of California,
again without California's consent. Each of these States might
*add* (or try to add) a few citizens for sentimental or honorary
reasons—say, all the living descendants of the Marquis de
Lafayette or of John C. Calhoun—but these are a trace element. (The very validity of such romantic additions would be
exceedingly doubtful, because it is Congress that is empowered to establish "an *uniform* rule of naturalization," and these
words are probably to be seen as preemptive. The Fourteenth
Amendment's confirmation of *state* citizenship should also be
taken, I think, as preemptive.) In the overwhelming main the
right to be and to call yourself a citizen of any State is not a
right conferred by that State, but a right bindingly ordained
as a matter of *national* constitutional law. It will be a more than
satisfactory approximation to say (leaving out of account a
handful of dubious oddities) that all citizens of Ohio are also
citizens of the United States who reside in Ohio.

This denial to each of the States of the right to choose its
own citizens might be looked on now as just another nail in
the coffin of the theory that our States are "sovereign." That
coffin can use all the nails it can get, because it yawns every
now and then, on some inauspicious midnight, to give up

its undead, clad perhaps in the senatorial toga of Calhoun. I will make more later of this national command of state citizenship; for now, it will do to say that unless this national command is utterly vain, it must have imported more than the right to put "citizen of North Carolina" after your name on a calling-card.

I have written of the "harmony" of these three cardinal commitments to a system of human rights. How does this last of the three enter that harmony?

The "privileges and immunities" of national citizenship can be, though they have not always been, treated in a straightforward manner. Even the lexicographer's art need not be contemned, at least as a source of suggestion of possibilities. As I write, I have turned around and looked up "privilege" in the 1939 edition of the of the unabridged Merriam-Webster that has somehow drifted through time into my possession (1939 is not far from the middle distance between us and the Fourteenth Amendment). I find that "privilege" can mean many things—a grant of a special right to a particular person, a grant of a patent or of a waiver, priority for a certain creditor, "primage" in the sea-law of goods-carriage, congressional or parliamentary immunity from arrest, the right of asylum or sanctuary, a "call, spread or straddle" on the stock market or the produce exchange. That's how words are—but none of these seems at all the sort of thing you would put in the lead clause of the treaty of peace after the greatest of wars up to its time, or that you would think of imposing on a state government as a right of its citizens.

There is one definition in my trusty dictionary that seems to rise to the great occasion:

> 3. Any of various fundamental or specially sacred rights considered as peculiarly guaranteed and secured to all persons by modern constitutional governments, such as the enjoyment of life, liberty, . . . [and] the right to pursue happiness.

*The entry then quotes, as its example, the very words of Section 1 of the Fourteenth Amendment.* I feel pretty safe in opting for that one, and not for a "straddle on the stock market," or "the grant of a manor," "ship's primage" or some concept of Roman law. Fortunately, lexicographers often have some common sense, and "3.", just quoted, fits a lot better in the context of this Amendment's language.

There is no reason for not taking the "privileges and immunities of citizens of the United States" (as our common-sense lexicographer evidently does) to include the "rights" set out in the Declaration of Independence. To avoid that conclusion, you have to drive a thin wedge between "citizens" and "people"; though in very much the greater part, they are the same human beings.

As this corpus of *national* "privileges and immunities" could have taken shape, under the deliberative processes of law, it could have become a visible and serviceable part of *national* law. In that character, it is a part of the supreme law of the land under Article VI, and under the view settled since *Marbury v. Madison,* a law superior to and controlling even Acts of Congress, as well as all other acts of the national government and any of its parts—and of course, under the express terms both of Article VI and of the Fourteenth Amendment, binding the States.

That would be all we really need on this score, but we have

just seen yet another way in which the States ought to be looked on as bound—a way not much attended to so far, but, I think, unquestionably solid. If you are a citizen of the United States and if you reside in Texas, then, by *national constitutional command* you are now a citizen of Texas as well. Texas has nothing to say about that. Now when a *status* is conferred on a person by the national Constitution, it can hardly be that the substantive consequences of that status do not go with the grant of the status, or that what these substantive consequences are to be is anything but a question of *national* law. The alternative would be that Texas citizenship, which the Fourteenth Amendment in its first sentence went to the trouble of granting and confirming to all citizens of the United States who live in Texas, is just an empty compliment, like a Kentucky colonelcy. (A compliment? Is it not rather an insult to the intelligence?)

The concept of "privileges and immunities" of citizenship "in the several States" is as old as the Constitution. (Article IV, Section 2.) But on the day the Fourteenth Amendment became law, every State entirely lost its right to exclude from its own citizenship, together (unless we live in Wonderland) with all "privileges and immunities" pertaining to such citizenship, *any United States citizen* residing within the State.

In one federal case, decided in 1825,[11] the "privileges and immunities" of *state citizenship* were very broadly defined. It may have been, though I think it unlikely, that a State might, before the great War and the Fourteenth Amendment, have been empowered to diminish these. But that's water that flowed under the bridge a long time ago. The Fourteenth Amendment quite surely redefined the position. The "privileges and immunities" of *state* citizenship are *now* fixed by national constitutional law unless the very clear grant, by that law, of state citizenship was a playful futility. Constitutional law does not deal in playful futilities.

So, as to the nation as a whole, there are "privileges and immunities." These are ample, and cannot be abridged or frustrated by any State. As to States, there are such "privileges and immunities" as go with citizenship in the State, this state citizenship being *mandated* by the national law of the Fourteenth Amendment.

Choice among these alternatives is perhaps not pressing; they take you to much the same place. Nor should this be surprising—since both are rooted in the same Declaration of Independence. One might add that there is nothing strange or paradoxical about the concurrence of national and state power in the securing of these "privileges and immunities." Such concurrence, on a much smaller scale, is a feature of the original Constitution, in the *ex post facto* and bill of attainder clauses of Sections 9 and 10 of Article I. As to all these concurrences of guarantees, large or small, the national interpretation has to prevail in case of conflict—because Article VI says so. Practically speaking, the guarantees of free speech and freedom of religion have been held to apply in just this way, though the Fourteenth Amendment "privileges and immunities" clause would furnish a much more acceptable basis than the one that has been used (see below, pp. 78–80 and 87–106).

Now many readers will know that these arguments were rejected or in part not reached, in the *Slaughterhouse Cases* in the Supreme Court in 1873,[12] ten years after Gettysburg. The arguments just above thus remain "visionary"—as "visionary" as

Abraham Lincoln's sacred prophecy at Gettysburg ("that this nation, under God, shall enjoy a new birth of freedom"). These first words of the Fourteenth Amendment brought his vision briefly into sight in law. The Supreme Court, by a five to four vote, waved that vision away—insofar as the newly confirmed moral unity of the American people, so dearly bought, could be waved away. Since we are examining the present real condition of American human-rights law, we have to take account of that destructive decision.

I will return to a detailed critical examination of the *Slaughterhouse Cases* in a later chapter. But for now we must not leave the matter altogether hanging. Let me deal as honestly and fairly as I can with the grounds on which the Court rejected any significant application of this clause of the Fourteenth Amendment to the States. I shall proceed schematically, assuring you that many questions will be dealt with later.

First, the Court points out that the Fourteenth Amendment recognizes that there is a *state* citizenship and a *national* citizenship, and that these two citizenships are distinctly referred to. So far, so good.

Secondly, says the Court, the mass of civil rights (before what we in the South used to call the "late unpleasantness"—that is to say, the greatest war, up to its time, in human history) was in the care of the States. One could argue very fundamentally about that, but that will be for later. Let us take it, *arguendo*, as broadly, though quite certainly not entirely, true. (This is not to concede, even *arguendo*, that there is anything anomalous or contradictory in the States' and the nation's both offering governmental protection for the same human rights.)

Finally, says the Court majority, it is incredible, whatever the bare words of the Fourteenth Amendment may seem to say, that the state power to define human rights within its territory "was intended" to be transferred to the care of the national government. Of this one may say, summarily:

1. The point is simply asserted, without any seeming attention to the awkward fact of the great Civil War. How can the Court pronounce, assertively and confidently, what "intention" may be projected as to the *future* adjustment of power in a national union that has been through such an experience?

2. The imputed "non-intent" sits more than uneasily in Section 1 of the Fourteenth Amendment, because the very next clause of that section, the famous "due process" clause, *does* radically and widely affect state independence as to *permissible procedures* for depriving any person of life, liberty or property. Of the procedures permissible, the States had been the sole judges. After the Fourteenth Amendment, there was and is an overriding national law of "due procedure." (There is also a new national law of "equal protection," touching and where needful changing every aspect of state law.) How could the Court conclude that *these* fundamental changes were *thinkable,* on the same day that the extension of general protection to a wide set of *substantive* privileges and immunities was *incredible?*

3. In an attempt to avoid an impression that it has entirely nullified the "privileges and immunities" clause, the Court does list a pitiful handful of "privileges and immunities" of national citizenship which *already existed* before the Fourteenth

Amendment. This preposterous list is really a *reductio ad absurdum* of the Court's holding.

4. To close a loophole, the Court is most insistent on the point that each State, being the authority responsible for the securing of civil rights, in its territory, has full power to diminish these at will, not giving any weight to the change in authority as to the holding of the "privileges" of *state* citizenship, that occurred when, under the first sentence of Section 1 of the Fourteenth Amendment, state citizenship itself was now enjoyed by national constitutional command.

5. Finally, the Court makes no attempt to solve or even to face the problem of the "privileges and immunities" of those who are "citizens of the United States," having been "born or naturalized therein," but who are not residents of any State—because they reside in the District of Columbia, or in the territories, or in foreign countries.

To condense all this, the upshot of the decision is: (1) that United States citizens as such have only a scrappy handful of *preexisting* "privileges and immunities" of *national* origin, and (2) that each of the States in which these citizens reside has full power to alter or to abolish altogether whatever "privileges and immunities" they have as *state* citizens. What a result for the Civil War! What a crumbly basis for *national* political morality! What a complete moral triumph for John C. Calhoun, who never won a battle in his own life. The decision simply cannot be right. I will return to this point later.

It takes some very picky reasoning not to read the words "citizens of the United States" to include "citizens of each of the States severally," and to claim for these directly the same privileges and immunities guaranteed to citizens of the United States. One dominant fact is that these are in very much the greater part the same people. "Law," as the late Jerome Michael liked to say, "is a practical subject."

The national privileges and immunities are set up not for ornament, but for a practical purpose—namely, that a valuable citizenship in a free society is to *prevail* in this nation throughout its territory. If this territory comes to consist (as it did not in 1868 or 1873) almost entirely of the territories of the States one by one, and the citizens of the States are the major part of the "people" of the United States one by one, these citizens will not be guaranteed the things promised in the charters of our freedom, if the States may whittle down those freedoms, those rights—free speech, immunity from religious coercion, the right to live with your orphaned grandchildren—contained in one hallowed phrase, "the pursuit of happiness."

The fact (an amazing one in view of the intervening great Civil War for national unity) is that, on the level of our highest values, this *Slaughterhouse* holding is a very close fit with the banefully "classic" doctrines of John C. Calhoun, the great heresiarch, on the relative importance and worth of *national* citizenship (not very much) and state citizenship (nearly everything). The South may be said to have surrendered to John Marshall but the Supreme Court, in *Slaughterhouse*, surrendered to Calhoun. As a bridge into the next chapter, let me remind you that most successful and unsuccessful claims of infringement of human rights are made *against the actions of state and local governments.* John Marshall, in an early opinion on a claim of right by Indians, remarked with certain truth that the people most likely to infringe against your human rights are not the people who are far away, but are those nearest you, where getting at you is easy. Attempts at book-banning, *de jure* or *de facto* racial segregation, the prohibition of the teaching of evolution, the censorship of movies, the regulation of clothing, are things mostly undertaken by state and local governments. (An apparent exception exists in cases where the national government runs, as in the District of Columbia, something that amounts to a local government.) If the national "privileges and immunities" are not good against the States and their subdivisions—if *that* is the Catch-22 of our boasted national regime of freedom—then we have set up nothing but a beeswax simulacrum of a free nation, for in fact and in truth, as to almost all its territory, and almost all its people, it is a *nation* that does *not*, as a *nation*, "secure" human rights. It was just that kind of result that the Civil War was in the deepest sense fought and won to prevent. Such a concept is death to Abraham Lincoln's sacred prophecy, at Gettysburg, that this nation, *as a nation*, might have a "new birth of freedom."

The purpose of this chapter has been the introduction, no more than that, of an important theme—that a satisfactory fundamental legitimization of an open-ended series of open-textured human rights, the only thing that can cover the lives of real people in their infinite variety and in their unforeseeable development, can be seen to flow from our basic commitments. A few collateral observations must be made.

First, I invite you to believe I have chosen the components of this foundation carefully, and that I have expounded each of them on the basis of the words chosen by the original expressers to be the words of authority. I think that is all we need, and that we proceed most safely if we respect those very words, following them as far as they may legitimately lead us.

If the words of the applicable passages in the Declaration of Independence, of the Ninth Amendment, and of the Fourteenth Amendment's "citizenship" and "privileges and immunities" clauses were really dark, if they could be interpreted only by esoteric reason, or by "narrow verbal criticism," or by an attempt to piece together the informally and sometimes delphically expressed subjective "intents" of selected people long gone, in regard to questions they did not face, then we might have to enter on such inquiries—of proven inconclusiveness though they be. If the Ninth Amendment and the relevant parts of the Fourteenth Amendment were nothing but "ink-blots," giving no guidance to the mind, whether of judge or of citizen, then we might have to set, generation after generation, such Rorschach tests as recurrently anxious scholarship could devise *and of course endlessly revise.* But I earnestly invite you to consider whether the words actually agreed to as the actual operative words are really all that obscure in character.

The Declaration of Independence asserts that all people have the "right" to "the pursuit of happiness." What would make you think that that phrase—given its full generality of expression and its close collocation to "liberty," and considering that it is a "right" not to "happiness" (which no political organization can give) but to the *"pursuit"* of happiness— meant anything in 1776 that it does not mean now? It is true that some change has perforce taken place in judgments as to the chance that happiness will result from different choices of means of pursuit. Perhaps more people then than now thought that devotion to religion was the best road to happiness. But if the word "pursuit," directly associated with "liberty," implies the right to *choice of means*, there is no change in *general* meaning. Or how would you state the distinction, and support its reality?

Passing to the Ninth Amendment, the "ink-blot" Amendment *par excellence*, it evidently calls for expounding the meaning of the phrase "other ["rights"] retained by the people." But what could make you loath to turn, for this necessary purpose, to the most apt source, the Declaration, where the rights of humankind are set out, just thirteen years before the Ninth Amendment was proposed and transmitted to the States? Why keep worrying around with the same old ink-blot, when there is so ready (indeed so unavoidable) a route of escape.

When we get to the word "privileges" in the Fourteenth Amendment, we do have a somewhat technical word. So it was and is, as I have shown, in many curious contexts, none of them seeming to have anything to do with any imaginable objective of this Amendment. But as my lexicographic material has just showed, there is one accepted and common meaning of the word "privileges" which is judged (presumably by an apolitical lexicographer) to fit the *very words* of the Declaration of Independence—including the "right to the pursuit of happiness."

What in the world is the problem? The fit of the Declaration to the Ninth Amendment seems natural enough. The fit of the Declaration—as now incorporated in the Ninth Amendment—is the first thing that strikes the mind of a person whose professional job is to give apt illustration of the use of the word "privilege." What drives people to pass over all this? Particularly lawyers?

I am sure that the result of my line of thought—a generalized and endlessly productive system of human rights—is in itself repellent to many people, however clearly the authoritative words I have been addressing may seem, in their harmony, to lead to that result. There is a myth that lawyers must think small, even meanly, or lose the aura of professionalism. As in all other matters, we should think at the level of magnitude proportioned to the problem. Insistence on thinking small veils the largest facts from view. If we are to have a true *system*, a productive system of human rights, we have to commit ourselves to thinking large. If we are to take seriously the noble words of our past, we must pronounce them with emphasis and without apologetic hesitation. After all, in doing this we risk a good deal less than being hanged, drawn, and quartered.

Very closely akin to the fear of ampleness of thought is the fear of generality. Our national commitment to human rights starts with generalities: liberty, the pursuit of happiness. What is sometimes forgotten is that all law works from level to level, with commitment to great general principles that have to be worked into practice through insight and experience. This is true, for example, of our commitment to "freedom of speech." That concept must be worked into life at all levels of generality, and each level has its own problems of prudence and balance. The same pattern can be expected in our commitment to the right to the "pursuit of happiness," which must be worked out in the same way. But neither of these things means that neither "freedom of speech" nor "the right to the pursuit of happiness" can be worked into law.

This is a characteristic not just of one kind of law, or of one level of generalization in the commitment which we must go on trying to apply. Take the law of contract. It rests on acceptance of the vast principle that contracts are to be looked on as binding, and are to be enforced. The actual working-out of this principle is in lower levels of law. A contract to submit to a disfiguring mutilation would not be enforced. A contract by which a shipper by sea gives up his right to the carrier's diligence in care of the cargo is widely disallowed and treated as invalid, both by case law and by statute law. The definition and scope of a doctor's obligation to his patient cannot be freely manipulated by contract. And so on *ad infinitum*. None of this means that contract law is not law. It just means that the first principles of contract law are not absolutes. Of course no one could have an absolute right to enforcement of any contract, or to say anything regardless of its untruth or of the noxious character of the means used. But the general principle of contract law has serious reality and wide relevance in law. So does the principle of freedom of speech. Much flows from each of these principles, though not everything flows from them that they might seem to promise, if one didn't know how law of all kinds is developed on different levels.

This chapter can appropriately end with a condensed and rather assertive summary of my chief pattern of thought for this book and for the fresh beginning of our human-rights law. Each of the following points requires thought and discussion; each has already been given some of these things, and will get more—besides some collateral shoring-up. But the following list will serve to focus the mind on the points around which everything else in this book revolves:

1. The 1776 Declaration of Independence commits all the governments in our country to "securing" for its people certain human rights, "among which are life, liberty, and the pursuit of happiness." These are the certified cardinal values of our political morality. It is a separable question whether they are also "law," available as such. (I think they are.)

2. The 1791 Ninth Amendment to the Constitution is unmistakably "law," and unmistakably rejects the idea that a human right, to be valid in law, must be enumerated (or explicitly named). The Amendment does not say which rights are the "others retained by the people," and are therefore not to be disparaged or denied (what a silly thing to think it could have done that!). But the Declaration of Independence, uttered a mere thirteen years earlier, supplies this lack in major part: There is no apter reference than the Declaration for clearing up the words "retained by the people," whether the Declaration itself be "law" or not. The Ninth Amendment is certainly "law." All governmental units—the national government, and by the consequences of the rule of construction it sets in place, the state governments with their subdivisions—are bound by it, as a matter of law, and therefore ruled by its incorporation by reference of the Declaration's words.

3. The "citizenship" and the "privileges and immunities" clauses of Section 1 of the Fourteenth Amendment form a complex whole.

Citizens of the nation are, by national constitutional command, also citizens of those states, respectively, wherein they reside. Since state citizenship is a nationally commanded status, the substantive incidents of such citizenship are to be governed by national law. *To be a citizen of the State wherein you reside is a privilege annexed to and flowing from national citizenship.*

These two paths of thought lead to exactly the same result—the enjoyment, by the citizens of each State (as well as by the citizens of the nation, who are mostly the same people), of national rights founded on the Declaration of Independence and on the Ninth Amendment (see point 2, above).

The national privileges and immunities of citizens of the United States are similarly derived and defined, and the States are forbidden to "abridge" them.

It is only against this point 3 that there is any precedent even technically binding—the *Slaughterhouse Cases* of 1873. This decision will be thoroughly discussed later. It is my own view that no sorrier opinion was ever written than the *Slaughterhouse* opinion, and that that case should be thrown into the rustiest trash-can of legal history. I have no illusion that this will be politically easy, but I think it is intellectually and technically easy.

Now the only thing I will add about this summary is that, if one shows it to a lawyer who, like most lawyers, has unequivocally (and often unthinkingly) accepted the most astounding, even scandalous, fact in American legal history—the consigning of the Declaration of Independence, the Ninth Amendment, and the Fourteenth Amendment "privileges and immunities" and "citizenship" clauses to virtual oblivion—that lawyer will smile tolerantly. This whole book is about the total unsupportability of these conventionally sanctioned attitudes of thought. I want you, now at least, to believe that I intend with the highest seriousness the proposals I am making for bringing home to their deserved positions of primacy these most precious of our treasures, forming our eternal tri-partite and harmonious commitment, as a nation, to a *general* system of human rights.

And remember, as this lawyer you are talking to politely smiles, that the very great majority of "sound" lawyers, when I was already well grown and then some, thought that the segregation of blacks, by law, from cradle to grave, and the "white primary," were "perfectly legal."

*Chapter 2*

# HUMAN RIGHTS
# AND THE
# STATES

In 1990, in a talk given in Moscow, I made what I commend to you now as the cardinal point about the place of our States in the American scheme of human rights. It is, incidentally, the most important general point about human rights in America. Because of the particular topic ("Glasnost") that had been assigned me, my thoughts were mainly directed to the human right of free speech, but the point is one of general applicability, and of a truth that goes to the life of real human rights in our country:

> In the United States, the right to free expression, if it is to be enjoyed in the real world, has to be guarded (like all American human rights) within the structure of what some of us have called "federalism"—the *coexistence*, in as good as every square foot of the country, of two governments, the national government and the government of some State. Free expression might be guaranteed in the most absolute and efficient way against *infringement by national law*—and still, *if there were no national guarantee of free expression, good against the States*, you might live all your years in dread of going to

prison for publishing or even owning a book dealing favorably with Socialism. The nation would not be in practical truth a free nation. There is no advantage, believe me, in going to a state prison rather than to a national prison.

Now it is true that most or all of our States have in their own constitutions some protection of free speech. But these protections—not being *national* law—would by themselves be subject to final interpretation by *state court* judges, most of whom are popularly elected, in decisions not reviewable in the *national* courts. And a state constitution is freely amendable by the legislature and the people of the State; in California, for one huge example, the state constitution may be and has often been amended by popular referendum.

If, as a last resort, you think this represents only a theoretical danger—that our States would never do bad things about free speech—then you ought to read a few of the hundreds of cases in which they have attempted suppression of speech of many kinds, including explicitly political speech. In this respect, they have shown far more imagination, over a much wider range, than the national Congress.

The upshot is that if we had no general national law binding the States to respect freedom of speech, enforced in the national courts, we would in no way be sure of at all enjoying this freedom, virtually anywhere. (This, I say again, is true of all human rights in the United States; without, for example, a national constitutional rule protecting the freedom of contraception against *state* violation we would not have freedom of birth-control and family planning, in this country, except where the States one by one chose to grant it from time to time. If none of them chose to grant it, we wouldn't have it anywhere—except in the District

of Columbia, a national enclave—or I guess maybe in our
Post Offices, where the question does not usually come
up.)

It is well to mention, too, that "state law" means not only
the formal law of a whole State, but also the ordinances put
in place by cities and other subdivisions of the State, and
the actions of State judges and other state officials, including police.[1]

Since this book is in large part about the force in law of "unnamed" human rights—such rights as are not specifically
named in the Constitution or its Amendments—let me go a
little deeper into the predicament we would be in, even as to
free speech and freedom of religion, if we had to cite a constitutional text protecting these prime human rights *against the
exercise of state and local power* before we could justify interpos-
ing a shield against such *state and local infringement*. Anybody
who can read can read that the First Amendment to the Constitution, where these rights are "enumerated," forbids their
infringement only by the *national Congress*. I shall later consider
more fully the manner in which this very plain textual limitation of the force of the First Amendment guarantees has
been surmounted (or clambered over in the dark) to bring
them to bear against the States. At this point we can just note
that, however you look at it, the explicit textual guarantees
even of expressive and religious freedom do not, in their own
terms, apply to the States at all.

But this illustration only dramatizes, perhaps just a little,
the fix we would be in if *other* valuable human rights were not
protected against *state* power, unless such rights were explic-

itly named. The pervasive and ineluctable fact is that power may be divisible, but the personhood of each human being is not so "divisible" as to make it possible for a person to be "free" when looked on as a subject of national power, while "unfree" as a subject of state power—free to marry at any age over eighteen, when considered as a subject of national power, but headed for a state prison if one marries before turning thirty-five, if a state law forbids that except when three solvent sureties make bond that no offspring of the proposed marriage shall become public charges. It is the same human being, and state prison is no better than national prison.

*This* is the lurking Catch-22, the treacherous snake-in-the-grass, in "Our Federalism," with respect to our guaranteeing human rights as "one nation indivisible."

Following the plan of Chapter 1, that of setting out a fresh foundation for human rights in American law, I shall consider in this chapter the applicability of that course of thought to the judging of actions of the States. What has this three-part scheme to do with the States?

Are they not bound by the three commitments that I have invoked in the first chapter: the Declaration of Independence, the Ninth Amendment, and the privileges and immunities clause of the Fourteenth Amendment?

First, as to the Declaration: This transcendentally solemn act was assented to by the representatives of all the States then in being; States later joining are of course equally bound. The language of the Declaration speaks to the duty of *governments in general* to "secure" the rights to life, liberty, and the pursuit of happiness—with no distinction as to the levels or partitions of government so obligated.

I have already committed myself to the view that the Declaration should be looked on as embodying "law" in the full sense. If it does so, then of course it binds the States as a matter of law, and controls state law.

But, as I have said above, you need not make up your mind on that question, if you accept the closely related view that the most natural reference, by far, of the Ninth Amendment, in the phrase "others retained by the people," is to the "rights" already named (just thirteen years before) in the Declaration. I remind you of the close fit between the language of these two documents, of the propriety of taking the Ninth Amendment's words "others retained by the people" as referring in large part to rights to be looked on as "retained" because they had already been designated as rights of the people by the Declaration, and of the virtual contemporaneity of the documents—separated as they were by an interval less than the one that now divides us from the middle of Reagan's first administration. The acceptance of that equivalency makes the words of the Declaration in effect a part of or (more accurately speaking) a prime subject of the rule of construction commanded by the Ninth Amendment, and therefore a part of the Constitution, and so a part of the "supreme Law of the Land," binding within and upon every State.

In the present context, concerning as it does the human-rights obligation of the States, the only Ninth Amendment question remaining is whether that Amendment in its terms applies at all to the States. The radical reference-point in the Amendment is to the "enumeration in the Constitution of certain rights." "Enumeration" of *some* rights is not to be "construed to deny or disparage others retained by the people." It is the fact that a number of rights, good against the States, *are* "enumerated" in the Constitution. It is hard to calculate the firm number of these. Some of the rights are resultants from explicit rules, such as the Article I designation of voters in elections for Congress, as those qualified by state law to vote for the more numerous branch of the State legislature; by irresistible inference, this generates a correlative *right* in the same people to vote for Congressmen. Some are direct and specific, like those collected in Article I, Section 10. At least one provision (Article IV, Section 2, clause 1) in the original Constitution is in quite general terms. The right of citizens and others to enjoy the benefit of the "full faith and credit" rule of Article IV, Section 1, is binding on every State. There are certainly enough such protections of rights in the original Constitution and in the Amendments that are *to all intents and purposes* part thereof, to put to flight the idea that there were and are therein few or no rights good against the States, and therefore nothing of that sort to which the Ninth Amendment could apply.

Moreover, the Ninth Amendment, like all prior and subsequent Amendments, is "to *all* intents and purposes . . . part of the Constitution" (see Article V). There is no reason why a rule of construction, such as that commanded by the Ninth Amendment, should not be held to prevail as to the "enumeration . . . of rights" in those *later* amendments (such as the immunity from sexual discrimination *in voting* forbidden in Amendment XIX), which, under the Ninth Amendment "rule of construction," should not be held to be grounds for "denying or disparaging" other rights validly derivable by any legally proper method, whether from structure or analogy, or otherwise. (It would be interesting to rework the cases dealing with the post–Civil War Amendments [XIII to XV] with this in mind.)

To sum up on this point: In its literal terms, the Ninth Amendment rule of construction does apply to rights guaranteed against state infringement, because that is how the Ninth Amendment designates and defines its own application. If there is any overpowering structural reason to the contrary, I should like to hear what it is, but I'll let those who believe in it phrase it and support it. I don't believe in it, and I would be at a loss to construct support for it. We ought to stop quibbling about our seminal national commitments.

Let us go on, then, to the third of our master commitments to human rights—the applicable clauses of the (1868) Fourteenth Amendment. For convenience, I'll quote these again:

> Section 1. All persons born or naturalized in the United States, and subject to the jurisdiction thereof, are citizens of the United States and of the State wherein they reside. No State shall make or enforce any law which shall abridge the privileges or immunities of citizens of the United States; nor shall any State deprive any person of life, liberty, or property, without due process of law; nor deny to any person within its jurisdiction the equal protection of the laws. . . .
>
> —
>
> Section 5. The Congress shall have the power to enforce, by appropriate legislation, the provisions of this article.

This Amendment was submitted to the States under the condition that no State that had joined the Confederacy could be readmitted to the Union without ratifying the Amendment. The parts of the Amendment of major and permanent significance are Sections 1 and 5, just quoted. Section 1 is therefore the salient, substantive provision of the treaty of peace ending our great Civil War. Its ratification was imposed on the rebelling States as the price of their reunion.

There are two distinct paths opened by the fact that not only *national* citizenship but *state* citizenship as well is enjoyed under the unmistakable command of this *national law.* I feel justified in stressing this again because conversations with students, even advanced law students, even some lawyers, have led me to think of it as a little-known fact. It's as though a cloud of unknowing covered these words in the Fourteenth Amendment. If I'm right on this, the cause may be that the States are so often referred to as "sovereign," and the power to designate the "sovereign's" own "citizens" is so commonly thought of as a power quintessentially pertaining to "sovereignty," that many people can't quite grasp what the Fourteenth Amendment so plainly decrees. Be that as it may, the fact is as it is: All or almost all the citizens of any State are (since 1868) citizens of that State because the Fourteenth Amendment says they are—not, I might add, that they "shall be," but that they "are."

So when we ask, at this turn in the argument, whether this command carries with it any human rights good against the so-commanded States, we are really asking whether the Fourteenth Amendment went to all that trouble just to do a vain thing—conferring a merely titular "status" of state citizenship that created no substantive consequences. If we cannot satisfy our minds with so lame and impotent a conclusion, then we have to ask what the rights of state citizenship are to be taken to be, *as a matter of national law.*

The first clue is that the phrase "privileges and immunities of citizens in the several States" occurs in the original Constitution:

> Article IV, Section 2. [1] The Citizens of each State shall be entitled to all Privileges and Immunities of Citizens in the several States.

In 1825, Supreme Court Justice Bushrod Washington, sitting as Circuit Justice, was confronted with a question about the meaning of the just-quoted provision. Did it render invalid a New Jersey law limiting to residents of that State the right to take oysters, clams, and shells in New Jersey waters? Rightly or wrongly, Mr. Justice Washington upheld the state statute, on the narrow ground that these mollusks in New Jersey waters were a part of the state's patrimony, in effect the "property" of its actual residents, the benefit of which the State might permissibly reserve to these residents. To reach a conclusion on this question, he had to consider what the phrase "privileges and immunities of citizens in the several states" *did* mean. His exposition, in *Corfield v. Coryell*, became classic:

> The next question is, whether this act infringes that section of the constitution which declares that "the citizens of each state shall be entitled to all the privileges and immunities of citizens in the several states?" The inquiry is, what are the privileges and immunities of citizens in the several states? *We feel no hesitation in confining these expressions to*

*those privileges and immunities which are, in their nature, fundamental; which belong, of right, to the citizens of all free governments; and which have, at all times, been enjoyed by the citizens of the several states which compose this Union, from the time of their becoming free, independent, and sovereign.* What these fundamental principles are, it would perhaps be more tedious than difficult to enumerate. They may, however, be all comprehended under the following general heads: *Protection by the government; the enjoyment of life and liberty,* with the right to acquire and possess property of every kind, [*552] *and pursue and obtain happiness and safety;* subject nevertheless to such restraints as the government may justly prescribe for the general good of the whole.[2]

Now do you see anything familiar within that description of the "privileges and immunities of citizens in the several States"? Of course you do. Justice Washington has been looking at the Declaration of Independence, which was proclaimed when he was a lad of fourteen, and which, for that reason, he probably could not see as being lost in the remote cuneiform antiquity that shrouds the Code of Hammurabi. (After all, two of the signers of the Declaration, Jefferson and John Adams, were still living in 1825!) "Life, liberty, and the pursuit of happiness" are right there in the Corfield opinion.

That lexicographer we encountered in the first chapter of this book (see p. 26 above) knew his business. It was natural almost to the point of inevitability that the famous words of the Declaration should be taken as supremely suitable to fill out and explain the words "privileges and immunities of citizens." This is not a conclusion that we, or the lexicographer, or Mr. Justice Washington, must strain and struggle to reach. It is a conclusion we would have to strain and struggle to avoid reaching. Why should we want not to reach it? It says all that is best about our nation. It makes a unity of our story.

A crucial and fundamental clarification in authority occurred with the passage of the Fourteenth Amendment. The rather convoluted wording of the Article IV passage might seem to a "poring man" to leave it open whether a state might *subtract*, from the substantive content of its own citizenship, some of the rights mentioned in Mr. Justice Washington's words. True, he speaks of these rights as having "been enjoyed at all times" by citizens of every State, he calls them "fundamental," and he says "they belong of right to the citizens of all free governments." But the *permanency* of that enjoyment might *just barely* not be thought protected, as against some State that might want to diminish these rights. This was perhaps not a likelihood, and it certainly would be puzzling in the face of the holding that these are the rights enjoyed under "all free governments," but it was a rarefied theoretical possibility before the Fourteenth Amendment.

But since the Fourteenth Amendment was ratified, the *status of being a citizen of a State* has been something firmly based on the *national* law of the Constitution. How trivial and how paradoxical it would be to think that some State might alter the substantive content of this grandest and most comprehensive of its obligations to its own people, who are also *our* people, part of *us*, part of "The People of the United States"!

This may be a point at which you wonder why I am insisting so strongly—and at such length—on something so obviously right, if I have been right in my contentions that precede its statement.

I have given it as my view that (treating such a question as ever new), we ought now to recognize that the Declaration of Independence has the force of law, and that the States are bound by the law of the Declaration.

I have also put forward the view that the Ninth Amendment must properly be looked on as referring to the rights set out in the Declaration, and that the Ninth Amendment must be construed as applicable to the States.

I have just now put before you the view that the *state citizenship* subclause of Section 1 of the Fourteenth Amendment carries within itself the command that the States treat their citizens (bindingly made such by the Amendment) in accordance with the privileges and immunities *of the Declaration,* if "citizenship" in a political body within the American system implies that that body must treat you in accordance with the Declaration. On the other hand, nothing in this thought impairs the generality and reach of the "privileges and immunities of citizens of the United States" in the Amendment, which, by virtue of its part of being the "supreme Law of the Land," becomes binding in and upon every State.

Since these lines of thought end up at the same place, why go through them all? Nobody ought to be shocked by these conclusions, because that is just about what Justice Washington said in 1825, less than fifty years after the Declaration went out. I am doing this because I want to bring you to see that the commitment of the American republic to human rights has depth in time and in the harmony of its precious components.

Consideration of the "privileges and immunities" of the Fourteenth Amendment brings us to yet another instance in this harmony, in this case bridging the state and the national obligation to "secure" human rights.

The Fourteenth Amendment gives authority to the idea that these "privileges and immunities of citizens of the United States" exist. What are *these* to be taken to be? What, indeed, except the very "rights" named in the Declaration of Independence? Is not this conclusion powerfully confirmed by the Preamble, wherein the *purposes* of the ordainment of the Constitution are stated: "To form a more perfect Union, *establish justice,* insure domestic tranquillity, *provide for . . . the general welfare, and secure the blessings of liberty* to ourselves and our posterity"? How could it be thought that these great ends could be accomplished unless the privileges of citizenship were borne up by *national* law? How else would there exist a national power to "secure" the rights of the Declaration? The obvious answer to these questions is the key to the interpretation, the filling with content, of the *Fourteenth Amendment* phrases. If not, what was the situation of the residents of the District of Columbia, or of citizens of the United States living in the territories, or abroad?

From this conclusion may be drawn innumerable obligations binding the *national* government—an open set of obligations. And the key point here is that the privileges and immunities clause of the Fourteenth Amendment expresses an open-ended series of rights, set up and recognized in this clause as inherent in *national* citizenship. What is the duty of the States respecting this corpus of human rights, established by "the supreme Law of the Land"?

*The States are not to use their general law-making power to "abridge" them.* Are not "the Judges in every State bound thereby, anything in the Constitution and Laws of any State to the contrary notwithstanding"? "No State" may "make [a] law" that on its face or in its operation nullifies, or in some way curtails or abridges the force, the authority, the *efficacy in practice* of some privilege or immunity of national citizenship. When we get that far, we are really up against the Supremacy Clause of Article VI.

> This Constitution, and the Laws of the United States which shall be made in Pursuance thereof; and all Treaties made, or which shall be made, under the authority of the United States, shall be the supreme Law of the Land; and the Judges in every State shall be bound thereby, any Thing in the Constitution or Laws of any State to the Contrary notwithstanding.

Let's go back to the illustration I began this chapter with. I have noted that the First Amendment free-speech guarantee, on its face, applies only to Congress' actions. But if the enjoyment of "liberty" and the right to the "pursuit of happiness" are "privileges and immunities" of national citizenship, and if liberty to speak is a liberty, and if the acquisition of knowledge and ideas are, to many at least, vital ingredients in happiness, then the State that infringed on these rights would be "abridging" a privilege or immunity of national citizenship, now very clearly made law by the Fourteenth Amendment. That idea goes all the way back to *McCulloch v. Maryland.*[3] After all, the Maryland law in that case did not directly and in terms violate a national law; what it did was to *interfere with the functioning of a system created by national law.* The prime system the United States exists to secure is a national regime of human rights.

In the light of all this, what is to be taken as the reference of the phrase "privileges and immunities of citizens of the

United States"? Can you imagine anything more silly and trivial than the reduction of this largest of our generalizations about the consequences of our universal common citizenship to a scrappy half-dozen or so of minor and inchoate rights, excluding almost everything of weight, and shutting off the view that seemed so natural to Justice Bushrod Washington— Declaration of Independence and all? The all but astronomical sublimity of Mount Rainier, speaking silently out to the far streets of Seattle, is reduced to the merest dusty trace of a molehill.

Well, you don't have to answer the question whether you can "imagine" such a thing, for that is exactly, and without exaggeration, the holding of the *Slaughterhouse Cases*,[4] decided by the Supreme Court of the United States in 1873. In the exact etymological sense, the Court *annihilated* the privileges and immunities of national citizens, insofar as these were to be seen as ordained by the Fourteenth Amendment.

I am not going to put you through very much case-analysis in this book. But I have to do it this time, because you cannot really understand the shoddiness of the professional foundations of our current human-rights law, unless you have an understanding of what happened in the *Slaughterhouse Cases.* This is probably the worst holding, in its effect on human rights, ever uttered by the Supreme Court. It's worth (and requires) some effort to understand it.

The bare facts were simple; they can be most handily stated by quoting from the first headnote:

The legislature of Louisiana, on the 8th of March, 1869, passed an act granting to a corporation, created by it, the exclusive right, for twenty-five years to have and maintain slaughter-houses, landings for cattle, and yards for enclosing cattle intended for sale or slaughter within the parishes of Orleans, Jefferson, and St. Bernard, in that State (a territory which, it was said . . . contained 1154 square miles, including the city of New Orleans, and a population of between two and three hundred thousand people), and prohibiting all other persons from building, keeping, or having slaughter-houses, landings for cattle, and yards for cattle intended for sale or slaughter, within those limits; and requiring that all cattle and other animals intended for sale or slaughter in that district, should be brought to the yards and slaughter-houses of the corporation; and authorizing the corporation to exact certain prescribed fees for the use of its wharves and for each animal landed, and certain prescribed fees for each animal slaughtered, besides the head, feet, gore, and entrails, except of swine.

The interesting question, for us, is whether this statute violated the "privileges and immunities" clause of the Fourteenth Amendment, as quoted above: "no State shall make or enforce any law which shall abridge the privileges and immunities of citizens of the United States . . . "

Of this Louisiana law the Court majority says, early in its opinion:

It cannot be denied that the statute under consideration is aptly framed to remove from the more densely populated part of the city, the noxious slaughter-houses, and large and offensive collections of animals necessarily incident to the slaughtering business of a large city, and to locate them where the convenience, health, and comfort of the people require they shall be located. And it must be conceded that the means adopted by the act for this purpose are appropriate, are stringent, and are effectual.

In common sense and in soundness of judicial practice, the case should have been decided and thrown out right there. If it was so clear, as it was to the Court and I think is to us, that this state law was a reasonable regulation of the practice of slaughtering—a practice necessarily and frequently regulated, and fraught with danger to the health and comfort of the people unless so located as to minimize these effects—then (if authority were needed for so obvious a thing), the statute would appear exactly to fit the passage the Court quotes with approval from *Corfield v. Coryell,* where Mr. Justice Washington added, to his comprehensive listing of the "privileges and immunities" enjoyed in our civilized society, the necessary words ". . . subject nevertheless to such restraints as the government may justly prescribe for the general good of the whole." The conclusion would be that, under the facts as stated and evaluated by this very Court, the reordering of the New Orleans slaughterhouse situation was well within the compass of this reservation. To claim that slaughtering animals wherever and however you want to is, under any tenable interpretation, a "privilege and immunity of citizens of the United States" was (I think it not too much to say) frivolous—even disgustingly so, if frivolity can disgust. No court faced with such facts has to jump at once to the most thin-aired level of discourse, and decide in a general way the most abstract question possible about this clause, settling silently and destructively such real questions as whether (for one among infinite such examples) the right to marry and have a family is a privilege or immunity guarded by national law against arbitrary state infringement. Or the right to have an important say as to the education of your children. Or the right to go to church or not to go to church, as you think best.

Questions like these, throbbing with real life, ought not to be decided when you have before you only a question about the right to unregulated slaughter of animals anywhere in town.

It would be interesting to know how this absurd case got selected as the one on which the *whole fate* of the solemn "privileges and immunities" clause was to be summarily (and mortally) settled. But the truth is that, having stated the facts of the case in such a way as to make any but one result inevitable, the Court yokes the subject of ubiquitous unregulated butchering to the whole lot of "privileges and immunities of citizens of the United States" and leads the clause itself lowing to the sacrifice.

The knife is sharp. On the basis of the most "narrow verbal criticism" in the literature, the majority of the Court dissects the wording of Section 1 of the Fourteenth Amendment:

> The next observation is more important in view of the arguments of counsel in the present case. It is, that the distinction between citizenship of the United States and citizenship of a State is clearly recognized and established. Not only may a man be a citizen of the United States without being a citizen of a State, but an important element is necessary to convert the former into the latter. He must reside within the State to make him a citizen of it, but it is only necessary that he should be born or naturalized in the United States to be a citizen of the Union.

> It is quite clear, then, that there is a citizenship of the United States, and a citizenship of a State, which are distinct from each other, and which depend on different characteristics or circumstances in the individual.

> We think this distinction and its explicit recognition in this Amendment of great weight in this argument, because the

next paragraph of this same section, which is the one mainly relied on by the plaintiffs in error, speaks only of privileges and immunities of citizens of the United States, and does not speak of the citizens of the several States. The argument, however, in favor of the plaintiffs rests wholly on the assumption that the citizenship is the same, and the privileges and immunities guaranteed by the clause are the same.

The language is, "No State shall make or enforce any law which shall abridge the privileges or immunities of citizens *of the United States.*" It is a little remarkable, if this clause was intended as a protection to the citizen of a State against the legislative power of his own State, that the word citizen of the State should be left out when it is so carefully used, and used in contradistinction to citizens of the United States, in the very sentence which precedes it. It is too clear for argument that the change in phraseology was adopted understandingly and with a purpose.

Of the privileges and immunities of the citizen of the United States, and of the privileges and immunities of the citizen of the State, and what they respectively are, we will presently consider; but we wish to state here that it is only the former which are placed by this clause under the protection of the Federal Constitution, and that the latter, whatever they may be, are not intended to have any additional protection by this paragraph of the amendment.

Perhaps the most striking thing about this analysis is that it skips past the fact that in overwhelming majority, the "citizens" of the States are the same human beings as "citizens of the United States." Everybody who is a citizen of the United States is a citizen of some State, unless that person does not reside in a State—and, even in that case, only so long as that person does not reside in any State, which he may at any time and without notice elect to do. With perhaps some bizarre exceptions, of more than doubtful legality, everybody who is a citizen of a State is a citizen of the United States. Every citizen of the United States who lives in a State is a citizen of that State as well. It's the same person in an only metaphysically different hat.

Another principal fallacy in the Court's reasoning is to be found in the word "transfer" in the following passage:

> [With] few restrictions, the entire domain of the privileges and immunities of citizens of the States, as above defined, lay within the constitutional and legislative power of the States, and without that of the Federal government. Was it the purpose of the Fourteenth Amendment, by the simple *declaration that no State should make or enforce any law which shall abridge the privileges and immunities of citizens* of the United States, *to transfer the security and protection of all the civil rights which we have mentioned, from the States to the Federal government?* And where it is declared that Congress shall have the power to enforce that article, was it intended to bring within the power of Congress the entire domain of civil rights heretofore belonging exclusively to the States?
>
> All this and more must follow, if the proposition of the plaintiffs in error be sound. For not only are these rights subject to the control of Congress whenever in its discretion any of them are supposed to be abridged by State legislation, but that body may also pass laws in advance, limiting and restricting the exercise of legislative power by the States, in their most ordinary and usual functions, as in its judgment it may think proper on all such subjects. And still further, such a construction followed by the reversal of the judgments of the Supreme Court of Louisiana in these cases, would constitute this court a perpetual cen-

sor upon all legislation of the States, on the civil rights of their own citizens, with authority to nullify such as it did not approve as consistent with those rights, as they existed at the time of the adoption of this amendment. *The argument we admit is not always the most conclusive which is drawn from the consequences urged against the adoption of a particular construction of an instrument.* But when, as in the case before us, these consequences are so serious, so far reaching and pervading, so great a departure from the structure and spirit of our institutions; when the effect is to fetter and degrade the State governments by subjecting them to the control of Congress, in the exercise of powers heretofore universally conceded to them of the most ordinary and fundamental character; when in fact it radically changes the whole theory of the relations of the State and Federal governments to each other and of both these governments to the people; the argument has a force that is irresistible, in the absence of language which expresses such a purpose too clearly to admit of doubt.

We are convinced that no such results were intended by the Congress which proposed these amendments, nor by the legislatures of the States which ratified them.

The discernment and enforcement of an ample substantive corpus of national human rights under the name of "privileges and immunities of citizens of the United States," would not produce a general "transfer," but would simply bring into clear view a *superior national law* of human rights, against which state dispositions would be tested for their lawfulness. This would be nothing but a new field for application of the Supremacy Clause of Article VI of the Constitution, already thoroughly familiar as the key provision in the structure of our nation. Each of the States had, in 1787 and in 1873, and still has, a law of contracts, prescribing in copious detail the requisites for the formation of contracts, and their remedial consequences. But all these state laws are subject, under the supremacy clause, to the Article I, Section 10 prohibition against any state law "impairing the obligation of a contract." Ordinarily state contract law goes its own way. But whether the "obligation of contract" clause is offended by some particular state law is a *national* question, finally decidable in the national courts. Similarly, real-estate transactions are generally subject to state law, but a national treaty may impose an outside rule on some classes of such transactions.[5] The escheat of property, on the death of the owner without heirs or a will, is ordinarily a state-law matter—but Congress has been upheld in imposing a different rule for a national purpose.[6] This is the normal balance of our so-called "federalism."

Moreover, the *Slaughterhouse* Court need have read only a few words further into Section 1 of the Fourteenth Amendment itself to see that general, sweeping changes in state-federal allocations of authority were *not* out of range on the very day the Fourteenth Amendment became law. No *State* is to deprive any person of life, liberty, or property *"without due process of law."* This command (leaving out of account for now its exceedingly questionable expansion into substantive fields, see pp. 90–93 below) is a *general* requirement of national law as to the fairness of procedure in state civil·and criminal cases and in other actions of the States. It has begotten and continues to beget illimitable questions as to the adequacy of state procedures. The application to the States of the Fourteenth Amendment "privileges and immunities" clause would similarly have begotten innumerable special problems. But there would have been no question in the latter case any more than in the former of turning over, "transferring," the normal tasks of the States in administering civil and criminal law. What was involved in the "due process" field, and what would be involved in the "privileges and immunities" field, is the subordination, wherever needful, of actions of the States to *national* standards—the Supremacy clause, as always, speaking the last word.

The same remarks may be made about the "equal protection" clause immediately following. Even if only applied to blacks (and it has been found impossible so to limit it) it states a general rule, applicable throughout the corpus of state law.

But the hugeness of these fallacies may well be thought to be no more shocking than the nose-thumbing insolence in the Court's final turning to the question, "All right, you may say that there *are* then no privileges and immunities of national citizenship? We'll show *you*":

> Having shown that the privileges and immunities relied on in the argument are those which belong to citizens of the ˌStates as such, and that they are left to the State governments for security and protection, and not by this article placed under the special care of the Federal government, we may hold ourselves excused from defining the privileges and immunities of citizens of the United States which no State can abridge, until some case involving those privileges may make it necessary to do so.

> But lest it should be said that no such privileges and immunities are to be found if those we have been considering are excluded, we venture to suggest some which owe their existence to the Federal government, its National character, its Constitution, or its laws.

One of these is well described in the case of *Crandall v. Nevada.* It is said to be the right of the citizen of this great country, protected by *implied guarantees* of its Constitution, "to come to the seat of government to assert any claim he may have upon that government, to transact any business he may have with it, to seek its protection, to share its offices, to engage in administering its functions. He has the right of free access to its seaports, through which all operations of foreign commerce are conducted, to the subtreasuries, land offices, and courts of justice in the several States." And quoting from the language of Chief Justice Taney in another case, it is said *"that for all the great purposes for which the Federal government was established, we are one people, one common country,* we are all citizens of the United States," and it is, as such citizens, that their rights are supported in this court in *Crandall v. Nevada.*

Another privilege of a citizen of the United States is to *demand the care and protection of the Federal government* over his life, liberty and property when on the high seas or within the jurisdiction of a foreign government. Of this there can be no doubt, nor that the right depends upon his character as a citizen of the United States. *The right to peaceably [sic] assemble and petition for redress of grievances, the privilege of the writ of* habeas corpus, *are rights of the citizen* guaranteed by the Federal Constitution. *The right to use the navigable waters of the United States,* however they may penetrate the territory of the several States, *all rights secured to our citizens by treaties with foreign nations,* are dependent upon citizenship of the United States, and not citizenship of a State. One of these privileges is conferred by the very article under consideration. It is that a citizen of the United States can, of his own volition, become a citizen of any State of the Union by a *bona fide* residence therein, with the same rights as other citizens of that State. To these may be added the rights secured by the thirteenth and fifteenth articles of amendment, and by the other clause of the fourteenth, next to be considered.

I summon the boldness to say that the Court would have done well to omit the final taunt of this "list." What the list painstakingly shows is that, in the Court's view, *nothing* was set up, or added, or created, or even newly recognized by the Fourteenth Amendment's "privileges and immunities" clause.

Think in detail about that list of the rights taken by the Court to be given by the great words of the first sentence of this Amendment:

1. A citizen of the United States has a right to leave a State without paying an exit tax. That was the 1868 case of *Crandall v. Nevada*, which is perhaps somewhat tendentiously understated in the just-quoted passage. It stated the law, in any case, *before* the Fourteenth Amendment came into effect— and rests on *no* constitutional text.

2. Such citizens have the right to "demand" the protection of the national government when they or their property are in a foreign country or on the high seas. (To "demand"? I have called this an "inchoate" right, or perhaps I should have said an "imperfect" right. In any event, such as it was it existed and was immune from state "abridgment," before the Fourteenth Amendment.)

3. They have the right to use the navigable waters of the United States. This was well-recognized *before* the Fourteenth Amendment.

4. They have the right "to peaceably [sic] assemble and to petition the government for a redress of grievances." This right was set up in 1790, in the Bill of Rights. (But see below for the puzzle created.)

5. They possess all rights secured to "our citizens" by national statute, by the Constitution itself, and by treaties with

foreign nations, such as the rights secured by Amendments XIII (that is to say, the right not to be a slave) and XV (the right to immunity from exclusion from voting on the ground of race), by Article I, Section 9 (the right to the writ of *habeas corpus*), and by the "other clause of the fourteenth, next to be considered" (the reference seems to be to the "due process" clause and the "equal protection" clause, though this is not entirely clear). Of course, all those are "rights" already secured by national law, without reference to the Fourteenth Amendment "privileges and immunities" clause.

Four or six times zero is zero. In the Court's view, the "privileges and immunities" clause *had no operational meaning.*

On this list, the four Justices dissenting in the *Slaughterhouse* case commented:

> If this inhibition [the privileges and immunities of the Fourteenth Amendment] . . . only refers, as held by the majority of the court in their opinion, to such privileges and immunities as were before its adoption specially designated in the Constitution or necessarily implied as belonging to citizens of the United States, *it was a vain and idle enactment, which accomplished nothing, and most unnecessarily excited Congress and the people on its passage.* With privileges and immunities thus designated or implied no State could ever have interfered by its laws, and no new constitutional provision was required to inhibit such interference. The supremacy of the Constitution and the laws of the United States always controlled any State legislation of that character. But if the amendment refers to the natural and inalienable rights which belong to all citizens, the inhibition has a profound significance and consequence.

In the case of all these "privileges and immunities" so proudly deployed by the Justices in the majority, this is a just comment. I have lumped together, as my own number 5, those of which this appears on the very face of things—the Article I right to *habeas corpus*, treaty rights, and all other rights granted by other parts of the Constitution and its Amendments; these are available as a matter of law to all citizens of the United States (as well as, one should add, to all non-citizens, where their interests are implicated) under the Supremacy Clause of Article VI of the Constitution. (It is worth remarking that the first, second, and third of the rights in the list are *not* "enumerated" in the text of the Constitution, but had already been taken to be rights of national citizens.)

Brief comment may be made as to *Crandall v. Nevada*. That case, striking down a state law interfering (even by a small exit tax) with travel from one State to another, was decided without reliance on the Fourteenth Amendment, or indeed on any particular text, but on grounds of the very nature and structure of the Union. It was nevertheless a case *based on* the Constitution (for it could be based on nothing else), and in its timing, and its non-reliance on the Fourteenth Amendment, it is just another illustration of the fact that, as interpreted by the *Slaughterhouse* majority, the Fourteenth Amendment "privileges and immunities" added nothing, not even the *in extremis* stabilizing force of a fifth wheel.

The right of a citizen to demand the protection of the national government against foreign actions is an elusive and incomplete right. It's hard to see how Nevada could interfere with it, especially if the "demander's" "life, liberty and property" are at risk "in a foreign country or on the high seas." But if Nevada had, in 1866, passed and attempted to enforce a state law making it a crime for a citizen of the United States to make such a "demand," or even, God save us, for an official of the United States to accede to such a demand *while in Nevada*, I don't think any Court at any time, with or without a Fourteenth Amendment privileges and immunities clause, would have hesitated to declare such a law void.

The one other example given by the majority (the right peaceably to assemble and to petition for redress of grievance) poses special problems, since it is in one sense a "named right" in the First Amendment, but (because that Amendment limits only "Congress") is *not therein "named"* as binding the States. The 1833 case of *Barron v. Baltimore* had held that the first eight Amendments, the so-called Bill of Rights, were not binding on the States. The textual reason for this is particularly clear in the case of the First Amendment, because (as we have seen) only *Congress* is disabled by the Amendment. But the puzzle of this "illustration" develops in yet another direction. If the assembly and petition rights are privileges and immunities of national citizens, then what about freedom of speech? It is protected in the same Amendment, and like the right of petition (which is only a form of free speech), it is a foreseeable element in the operation of the national government. I don't think the *Slaughterhouse* Court would have wanted to explore that. On the main point, there is no suggestion that the Fourteenth Amendment added anything to the right of petition, or that a state could validly have interfered with that right before the Fourteenth Amendment. What is shown, once again, is that in the Court's view the privileges and immunities clause of the Fourteenth Amendment has added nothing, that this great resounding clause, which seemed, just after the Civil War, to be summing up the moral result of that war—"one nation indivisible"; "a new birth of freedom"— actually had no operative force whatsoever, and was to be a mere dead letter.

This *Slaughterhouse* court says that to give broad substantive force to this "privileges and immunities" clause would be violative of some well-understood postulates about what (with reverential capitals that can be heard even when they are not written) is sometimes called "Our Federalism." (It has to be interesting that neither the word "federal" nor any of its derivatives and cognates occur in the Constitution.) It would be my answer that sweeping change in "Our Federalism" would not have been really surprising, after the end of what was up to its time the greatest war in human history, a civil war fought initially, continuingly, and, above all, to establish forever the national supremacy, as expressed in the Supremacy Clause of Article VI, of which an ample substantive content for national citizenship would be, as I have shown, just one more application. There is a tottering absurdity, which ought to be repugnant to every lawyer's mind, of triumphantly performing a conjurer's trick with the clause, in order to *annihilate* (it must have been anticipated for all time) every hope that such great words, used at such a moment in history, should mean anything at all, except a few little things that were already there when this Amendment became law. You know, that just can't be right. Al Smith's 1928 words seem dead on center: "No matter how thin you slice it, it's still baloney." Nobody before or since ever sliced it quite as thin as the *Slaughterhouse* Court did!

How would you like to try to explain, to a foreign person, that these words, so placed, simply had and have *no* substantive meaning? That (as this spoiler Court construed them) they neither *confirmed nor set up a general and generous national regime* of the privileges and immunities of citizenship in the United States?

This kind of thing is not unexampled in the wider world. Some forty years ago, I heard an official visitor from the Soviet Union speak of the rights of the citizens of *that* Union—freedom of speech and political action, no arbitrary imprisonment, and so on. He read out all the statutes and constitutional provisions; he did not detail the ways they used to bring them to nothing—the "Catch-22s."

I wonder whether any American representative has anytime lately made a speech in Russia, quoting the words "privileges and immunities of citizens of the United States" (rather sonorously, one imagines) as summing up, in a felicitous phrase of comprehensive reach, the whole essence of the American regime of human rights as a matter of law. If so, the chances are that this representative doesn't know any better. I think maybe you really have to be a lawyer to get inside the *Slaughterhouse* case enough to see how shabby, how sorry, it really was.

I'll add a couple of grace notes.

The Court, as courts so often do, surveys the "history" of the post–Civil War Amendments. Then it goes on:

> We repeat, then, in the light of this recapitulation of events, almost too recent to be called history, but which are familiar to us all; and on the most casual examination of the

language of these amendments, no one can fail to be im-
pressed with the one pervading purpose found in them all,
lying at the foundation of each, and without which none
of them would have been even suggested; we mean the
freedom of the slave race, the security and firm establishment of that freedom, and the protection of the newly-
made freeman and citizen from the oppressions of those
who had formerly exercised unlimited dominion over him.
It is true that only the fifteenth amendment, in terms, men-
tions the Negro by speaking of his color and his slavery.
But it is just as true that each of the other articles was addressed to the grievances of that race, and designed to
remedy them as the fifteenth.

Why in the world did the Court think such a set of considerations bore on its decision with respect to the "privileges
and immunities" clause of the Fourteenth Amendment? Is
there any suggestion, anywhere, that that clause applies to and
benefits only *blacks?* Or benefits them especially? Was such a
question presented in this case? No. This is just dust thrown
in the eyes. Having at such length indicated a tender concern
for black people, does or can the Court in any way apply that
concern to this case? No, race is not in the "privileges and immunities" question in this case. Whatever else it is, *Slaughterhouse* is not a race case.

There was one real danger. The Congress that had passed
the post–Civil War Amendments, and the early Civil Rights
Acts, might at some time take some action under the national
"privileges and immunities" clause that would be helpful to
blacks, if that Clause were to grow real teeth.

The Court needn't have worried. Some such laws were actually passed. But the Supreme Court pretty well did them all

to death. If you will look through the list (tabulated in the Annotated Constitution of the United States) of some twenty-five cases, in which the Court struck down Acts of Congress, through the whole nineteenth century—mostly after the Civil War ended—you will find that the majority of these decisions rested either on Bill of Rights procedural provisions or on infra-governmental grounds such as the relations of Congress to the Presidency or to the Judiciary. *Of the rest, the cases dealing with the affirmative powers of Congress, the only ones of any staying power or moment were the ones striking down or narrowing statutes protective of Negroes* (voting, lynching, public accommodations, and so forth). If you look over this list of cases, and consider that the latter half of the nineteenth century was a time of ample and Court-approved expansion of Congress' power (the last legal tender case, the proliferation of power in admiralty, the hanging of interstate commerce power on a mere "peg," as in *The Daniel Ball*), you are not going to be very far from the conclusion that the so-called "doctrine" of "strict construction" of Congressional power was generated by concern to keep black people in their place.

If you read Justice Bradley's opinion in the 1883 Civil Rights Cases, and some of his opinions on the "admiralty" power and on the power to make paper money legal tender, you will find it hard to believe that it's the same man. But his half-century well understood what "strict construction" was really meant to be in aid of. You may be surprised; the shade of John C. Calhoun would not be surprised—except perhaps pleasantly, on seeing that his doctrines as to national and state citizenship (that had seemed old crockery smashed to powder by the Civil War) had sprung up alive and well.[7]

The *Slaughterhouse* Court left another little message:

If any such restraint is supposed to exist in the constitution of the State, the Supreme Court of Louisiana having necessarily passed on that question, it would not be open to review in this court.

Remember the quotation from Mr. Justice Washington's opinion in *Corfield v. Coryell*[8] which the *Slaughterhouse* Court calls *"the first and leading case"* on the content of state "privileges and immunities." The *Slaughterhouse* majority *closes the quotation* and goes out on a track of its own, concerning the Article IV clause:

> The constitutional provision there alluded to did not create those rights, which it called privileges and immunities of citizens of the States. It threw around them in that clause no security for the citizen of the State in which they were claimed or exercised. Nor did it profess to control the power of the State governments over the rights of its own citizens.
>
> Its sole purpose was to declare to the several States, that whatever those rights, as you grant or establish them to your own citizens, or as you limit or qualify, or impose restrictions on their exercise, the same, neither more nor less, shall be the measure of the rights of citizens of other States within your jurisdiction.
>
> It would be the vainest show of learning to attempt to prove by citations of authority, that up to the adoption of the recent amendments, no claim or pretense was set up that those rights depended on the Federal government for their existence or protection, beyond the very few express limitations which the Federal Constitution imposed upon the States—such, for instance, as the prohibition of ex post facto laws, bills of attainder, and laws impairing the

obligation of contracts. But with the exception of these and a few other restrictions, the entire domain of the privileges and immunities of citizens of the States, as above defined, lay within the constitutional and legislative power of the States, and without that of the Federal government. Was it the purpose of the fourteenth amendment, by the simple declaration that no State should make or enforce any law which shall abridge the privileges and immunities of citizens of the United States, to transfer the security and protection of all the civil rights which we have mentioned, from the States to the Federal government?

If you look back and carefully read the *Corfield* quotation of 1825 (above, pp. 49–50), characterizing the "privileges and immunities" that Mr. Justice Washington believed to be those referred to by that phrase in Article IV, Section 2, you must at this point feel what may with extreme charity be called a jarring dissonance. Justice Washington (in what this *Slaughterhouse* court actually calls the "great and leading case" on the subject) sees the "privileges and immunities" of citizens in the several States as "fundamental"; they *"belong of right to the citizens of all free governments."* They include the Declaration of Independence, through to "the pursuit of happiness" *under that name.* Yet to the *Slaughterhouse* Court their "entire domain" lies all but totally within the power of the States.

That conclusion, once again, takes *no account* of the fact that, under the Fourteenth Amendment, the status of being a *state* citizen is a status bindingly ordained and confirmed by national constitutional law. If this *national* ordainment of *state* citizenship had just been omitted, then the "privileges and immunities of citizens of the United States" would have stood full-bodied and independent, because the conjurer's trick which made them antithetical to, and in a zero-sum game with, the "privileges and immunities" of the *very same people* as state citizens would have had nothing (instead of next to nothing) to rest on.

The lexicographers for the letter *P* would have had excellent illustrations for "paradox" and "perversity." They still do, as the text actually stands. The Court's conclusion goes directly against what would normally be thought the consequence of making the enjoyment of *state* citizenship a thing recognized and confirmed by *national constitutional law.*

Now look what they've done here—whether adroitly or by baneful instinct, who can say? The words I have emphasized stamp out any expectations formed around the just-quoted part of the *Corfield* opinion. In the face of the wholly new fact that state citizenship was confirmed as a national right by the Fourteenth Amendment, the Court may have thought (or at least dimly feared) that this new status of being a state citizen, having become something conferred by the national Constitution, might naturally be thought to be governed in its substance by national law. So they paused to step on *that!*

This was the *same* Court that at the same time was moving toward solidifying commitment to the idea, now black-letter law, that the mere grant to the federal judicial courts, in Article III of the Constitution, of judicial jurisdiction over "all cases of admiralty and maritime jurisdiction," was ground for the recognition and creation of a national system of substantive maritime law, binding on the States.[9] That was a much larger leap than it would be to conclude that the national *establishment* of state citizenship (not the mere mention thereof) implies a nationally protected *content* of such citizenship. The federal courts could have decided maritime cases on the basis of *state maritime law*, just as they do in many other cases governed by state law, though that would have been inconvenient. To read the command that huge numbers—nearly all—of national citizens should be citizens of the States wherein they reside, as leaving to the States the substantive consequences of one's being a state citizen, would be a total nullification of the very grant just given. The brighter sixth graders would have learned to smirk when reciting the words "one nation indivisible, with liberty and justice for all."

So that is *Slaughterhouse*. The opinion[10] blows a kiss at the recently freed slaves. That kiss was the kiss of death, as later cases that *did* affect black people showed, but it was blown from a long distance, since the *Slaughterhouse* case, in its central focus, had nothing to do with race, and the decision could therefore in no way be beneficial to black people. The only logical application of this historical stuff to the "privileges and immunities" question would have been to hold that, since the Court saw all these Amendments as being for the benefit of black people, and since the plaintiffs weren't black, the "privileges and immunities" clause, as to these plaintiffs, means nothing. But the Court did not choose to pursue this logic, because of course they were not saying, heaven forfend, that there is a special class of enforceable national "privileges and immunities" for black people. Instead, the *Slaughterhouse Cases annihilated* the "privileges and immunities" clause as a whole and in the most general terms, as to white and black alike. (It was a cost-free blown kiss.)

After this polite genuflection toward the black "beneficiaries," the Court gets on with its work of annihilation, even to the length, as I have just shown, of trying to cut off the reliability of benefit from the new *national* basis of *state* citizenship. It turns out nobody is to benefit incrementally in any way from the privileges and immunities clause. The Court even speaks with horrified disapproval of the possibility that Congress might deal with the substantive content of national citizenship—though, as a new matter, I should have thought that such Congressional action would be a power of sovereignty, as is the power to make paper money of the United States legal tender. We have here to deal with something more important than legal tender—the worth, one hundred cents on the dollar, of our own original national commitment to *secure* by law the human rights of us all and of those to come.

When all is said, the question whether the phrase "privileges and immunities of citizens of the United States" is full of meaning, or empty of meaning, has to be settled on the basis of competing alleged absurdities.

The Court puts the case wholly upon what it sees as the all but ineffable radicalness of the change proposed by those who would give this new and ample substantive meaning to this clause. That the case is put by the Court solely on that basis is clinched by the last sentence in a passage I have quoted: "We are convinced that no such results *were intended* by the Congress which proposed these Amendments, nor by the legislatures of the States which ratified them." This sentence states a bare conclusion about the minds of the members of both Houses of Congress and the members of the legislatures of three-quarters of the States. No evidence whatever is advanced, except the sheer implausibility of most people's wishing for so radical a change. (I am a bear on so-called legislative history, which, as I have sampled it, is chronically multifarious and inconclusive, particularly on such a great question as the present one, about which so much was said. But I believe that if I were going to announce my conviction on this "unthinkability," as the one and only ground for this savagely destructive decision, I would try to scare up something along the line of material evidence of the short statement of my conclusion as to the "did-not-intend" of a great many political people in far-flung places, and even of the people at large. I might even have tried to assemble some support, more than just my own assertion, that the settled institutions of the Republic would be shaken to their foundations if the meaningful privileges and immunities clause, rather than the meaningless one that was sanctified by the Court in *Slaughterhouse*, were to become law.)

The *Slaughterhouse* Court very greatly exaggerated the magnitude of the revolution it feared, or feigned to fear.

First, a real live "privileges and immunities" clause, as opposed to a waxen simulacrum, would be no more (and no less) than a new (or newly recognized) body of national law, developing as law develops, and binding as all national law is supremely binding. Such a body of law would fit in without any strategic theoretical change.

Secondly, such a body of human-rights law, national in authority, would not even in its content be wholly new. There were already explicit limitations on state power over human rights questions, culminating in the Thirteenth Amendment's abolition of slavery. Important and comprehensive *procedural* limitations ("due process of law") on the States were entering the Constitution in the very same section of the Fourteenth

Amendment, as was an "equal protection" clause applying, whatever its substantive scope might turn out to be, to *all* state laws. More such provisions, binding the States generally, were to come in the next few decades. A living "privileges and immunities" clause would have been just one in a series of national laws protecting human rights against any contrary dispositions in state law. Such a development, moreover, is deeply rooted in earlier history—in the commitments of the Declaration of Independence and of the Ninth Amendment. There is no question here of wrenching diastrophic change. The clause would have fitted into the structure of the Constitution, and into a process already in train within that structure.

Thirdly, but on a different and a larger view, what is all this astonishment about? The country had just been through one of the most painful and bloody wars in human history. As the Court recognizes, that war was rooted in that ultimate denial of human rights, slavery. About a third of the American States had fought not only to preserve this institution, but to spread it to the Western territories; in this grand design they had been abetted by the Supreme Court itself, in a decision handed down some dozen years before the Fourteenth Amendment passed. They also (and as a corollary) bitterly denied the national power over them, and gave their own last full measure of life's blood and property to make that denial stick. How strange would it really be that the victorious nation should address itself in a newly serious way to ensuring that human rights were to be thoroughly protected, in the future, by national power?[11]

This book is haunted by the heroic, brooding figure of

Abraham Lincoln. So much is plain from the Dedication and the Afterword, as well as throughout.

But as I have read and reread the manuscript of the whole book, and especially of this chapter, I have realized that in a quite different sense, another figure haunts the work—the figure of John C. Calhoun. I seem sometimes to have dated occurrences, even when they have nothing to do with him, by the date of his death. I have chosen to conjecture that the grisly undead corse of "states rights" rises ever and anon on midnight, wearing his senatorial toga. I have imagined him as a person all of whose descendants are sought to be given honorary citizenship in some imaginary State. All in all, it's a lot of Calhoun for such a short book.

I didn't start with the idea that Calhoun was a subject. The thought that he was playing a part came to me fully formed when I was rereading, for perhaps the tenth time, Mr. Justice Field's dissent in the *Slaughterhouse Cases*. This is the passage that arrested my attention, as I thought about its full implications:

> The first clause of this [i.e., the Fourteenth] amendment determines who are citizens of the United States, and how their citizenship is created. Before its enactment there was much diversity of opinion among jurists and statesmen whether there was any such citizenship independent of that of the State, and, if any existed, as to the manner in which it originated. With a great number the opinion prevailed that there was no such citizenship independent of the citizenship of the State. Such was the opinion of Mr. Calhoun and the class represented by him. In his celebrated speech in the Senate upon the Force Bill, in 1833, referring to the reliance expressed by a senator upon the fact that we are citizens of the United States, he said: "If

by citizen of the United States he means a citizen at large, one whose citizenship extends to the entire geographical limits of the country without having a local citizenship in some State or Territory, a sort of citizen of the world, all I have to say is that such a citizen would be a perfect non-descript; that not a single individual of this description can be found in the entire mass of our population. Notwithstanding all the pomp and display of eloquence on the occasion, every citizen is a citizen of some State or Territory, and as such, under an express provision of the Constitution, is entitled to all privileges and immunities of citizens in the several States; and it is in this and no other sense that we are citizens of the United States."

Until I placed the quoted words from Calhoun's 1833 Senate speech alongside the result in the *Slaughterhouse Cases*, I had thought Calhoun to be simply a rather unappealing antiquity. He believed human slavery was a positive good. The energies of his later years went into strengthening the position of the slave States, with a view to protecting slavery. He espoused and expounded the doctrine of nullification of national laws by individual States. He regarded secession from the Union as the right of any State. He thought that all the national powers set forth in the Constitution should be "strictly construed." He supported the refusal by the Senate to receive petitions aimed at slavery, and the closing of the United States mails to abolitionist literature.

I think all those are positions that have not stood the test of time and reflection. I never hear anybody speak well of slavery anymore, though I cannot vouch for other people's secret thoughts. If anything can be settled by history and acquiescence, it is settled that state secession is not lawful. Some heady talk of "nullification" did surface some decades ago, but it never really got anywhere. "Strict construction" of the national powers was far from prevailing or nearly prevailing even in Calhoun's own century,[12] and now has no *principled* constituency. (How does partial-birth abortion become a *national* subject?) Once in a couple of decades, the Supreme Court may test these waters, but nobody can think the oceanic mass of national legislation is going to be reduced to a "strict-construction" puddle; after all, the banks want a *national* law that protects due-on-sale clauses in mortgages, and everybody wants the national government to act against kidnapping and even crime in the streets, and so on, *ad infinitum.* We actually have a fully empowered *national* government; I don't know why some people think that is a bad thing.

It is astounding, then, that the views on the nature and relations of national and state citizenship respectively of such a figure as Calhoun should be the prevailing law in the United States as to the all-important matter of human rights. On all his other views—secession, nullification, slavery, "strict construction"—Calhoun is nowhere.

Yet the *Slaughterhouse Cases* held:

1. That the "privileges and immunities" of citizens of the United States as such are a derisory handful of "rights," construed *stricti juris,* which had existed *prior* to the Fourteenth Amendment.

2. That the fundamental "privileges and immunities" enjoyed in this country flow entirely from the States one by one, and that the States, one by one, may validly diminish these within their own borders, as far as they see fit.

This is a pretty close tracking of the implications of the Calhoun position in the passage quoted above, on the relative worth and importance of national and state citizenship respectively, with respect to human rights.

All that can be asked is that you weigh and consider critically the reasonings in the *Slaughterhouse Cases*, in the light of the fact that the result of that decision preserves in the amber of the United States Reports very much more than a trace of Calhoun's 1833 opinions on citizenship, as quoted above. The *Slaughterhouse Cases* have never been overruled. It is therefore, *today* technically the law of this country that the "privileges and immunities" of its national citizenship are just as they were when Calhoun spoke of that citizenship disparagingly in 1833, and that the *fundamental* privileges of citizenship are those of *state* citizenship, bestowed by the *States* one by one on their own citizens, and changeable or destructible at the will of each State.

I will permit myself to say again, as I have said of other aspects of the *Slaughterhouse* decision: "You know, that just can't be right!"

I must report one further irony: In one way the Slaughterhouse opinion may be more Calhounian than Calhoun in its *definite* and *express* holding that each of the States may diminish and devalue the "privileges and immunities" flowing from its citizenship. I would be surprised, in view of the general drift of Calhoun's "states rights" thoughts, if he would not agree, but in a passage aimed only at expressing his contempt for the concept "citizen of the United States," he had no occasion to reach that question.

At least he does *not* misquote the language of Article IV, Section 2 (". . . *in* the several States"). The majority opinion in *Slaughterhouse* in quoting this section, substitutes the words ". . . *of* the several States" for ". . . *in* the several States," and repeats this change (*"of"* for *"in"*) in the immediately following quotation from Mr. Justice Washington's opinion in *Corfield v. Coryell,* where the quote is correct. Let me be clear about this. Justice Washington, in his opinion, correctly quotes the Article IV phrase, but in quoting Washington's opinion, the Supreme Court opinion in *Slaughterhouse* takes some pains to alter the phrase to its own incorrect version! This misquotation does not occur in the dissenting opinion of Mr. Justice Field.

I don't know what we can make of these rather surprising misquotations of a very short and in the context quite crucial passage in the Constitution. Maybe they were just in a hurry to get the deed done: ". . . 'Twere well it were done quickly."


Early in November of 1863, Lincoln was invited to come to Gettysburg on November 19, and there to speak words of dedication of the new cemetery for the soldiers who had died in the great battle. Accepting, he worked nearly ten days on the short speech he finally gave, which became one of the most revered utterances in our history. He had no speechwriters; he read his draft to no one. His alone was the sublime expression of hope that "this nation, under God, shall have a new birth of freedom."

Only five years later, only three years after his death, the action of Congress and of the nation in proposing and ratifying the Fourteenth Amendment, gave an apt and authori-

tative form of words to this hope and prophecy, in the "privileges and immunities" clause linked to the status of national
citizenship.

In the case we have been examining, the Supreme Court
struck down the vision expressed in Lincoln's prophetic hope.
But the words and the hope of Gettysburg are still there, for
use when we are ready.

## Chapter 3

# THE TRANSITIONAL
# FUNCTION OF
# "SUBSTANTIVE DUE
# PROCESS"

In the first two chapters, I have proposed an approach to American human-rights law based upon three cardinal commitments and on their mutual harmony: the Declaration of Independence, the Ninth Amendment, and the "citizenship" and "privileges and immunities" clauses of the Fourteenth Amendment, Section 1.

The scandalous truth is, as we have seen, that the first two of these have been allowed to sleep, almost without stirring, for two centuries—to my mind quite long enough—while the third was forcibly drugged into coma by a 5–4 vote in the Supreme Court, in the *Slaughterhouse Cases* of 1873; I have examined, just above, the footless scramble to judgment of that decision, which I invite you to think of as one of the most outrageous actions of our Supreme Court. One way or another, all three of these cardinal commitments to human rights have so far played virtually no part in our human-rights jurisprudence. What have we used instead, and with what results? With no acknowledgment of the force of these commitments, we have been left with a miscellany of legal techniques, intellectually insufficient to support a *general* regime of human rights.

We are speaking here of a complex legal development that circles and meanders, and never stoops to simplicity. This material can be organized only in approximation. But I think I can give you a good approximation of the lines of question and context.

There has been an influential school of thought—on the Court and outside it—that has had respect only for the specific Constitutional texts protecting more or less specific rights. Some Justices on the Court have from time to time talked and acted as though these texts were the only proper source for human rights enforceable as a matter of constitutional law—though we must notice that as good as no Supreme Court Justice in either of our centuries has been consistent in this.

Since this narrow textualism has found and still finds recurrent strong expression—sometimes of a condescending or even a bullying tone—it is a good idea to look seriously and in detail, as we have done, at the constitutional texts available. Where would we be if we faithfully adhered to this austere canon? This inquiry cannot of course of itself tell us whether it is the right canon. But it will serve to suggest something about whether that is a dead-serious question. This purely textual material deserves a close reading.

Aren't you a little surprised that the *whole* of original Constitutional protection, by specific naming, of human rights—even counting the first eight amendments—is so skimpy? Perhaps we shouldn't be. The central understood purpose of the original Constitution was to *constitute* a structured and empowered government. The people who did this created—in the four months of a hot Philadelphia summer, about eight decades before the publication of *The Origin of Species* and three or four decades before the beginning of the steam railroad—a system that has lasted over two hundred years, surviving great changes and the greatest of shocks.

As to human rights, the 1787 framers of the Constitution did do one endlessly important thing. In the bill of attainder and *ex post facto* provisions they staked out the *principle* that the document that *constituted* the nation was also a fitting place in which to establish *human rights*, in the sheer interest of justice and in forthright contradiction to what might be the majority will at any one time. Sometimes, when I have read those two provisions, I have felt the back of my neck tingle; together they are the holdfast cell of the great and still growing American principle, now imitated throughout the world, that in the very *Constitution* of a national government there may be fixed provisions for human rights, binding on the constituted government by the very same authority as the one that structured and empowered it. This was one of the great American political inventions of our seed-time. I don't know whether that long step called for courage, or whether like some vastly creative things (perhaps the wheel) it may suddenly have seemed obvious to everybody. Reflecting on that very alternative ought to stir our courage to go on in the building of a wider and wider edifice of constitutional human rights.

After all, the greatness of the original Constitution, in the sphere of human rights, must be seen to consist in this dazzling invention, rather than in the uses to which it was put in the document. These were and I think can be said to remain very few. We are walking around in the spaces of a nation which we believe to guarantee "liberty and justice for all," as a matter of constitutional law. But outside the realms of free expression and religion (and in those only as to the national power), our original constitutional text, even including the Bill of Rights, protects only a few limited and special substantive human rights. That is not a slight variation on the principles of the Declaration of Independence, but very nearly antipodal to them.

In the wake of the *Slaughterhouse Cases*, wherein the Court chloroformed the "privileges and immunities" clause of the Fourteenth Amendment, it came slowly to be seen, or perhaps tacitly acknowledged, or perhaps something even vaguer and less visible, that common justice, and implementation of the shared national value of freedom, required more than this, not only for religion and speech but for other rights as well, such as the right to marry and to have a family. This, it seems clear, generated the development of "substantive due process."

An early Supreme Court case is illustrative of this—*Chicago v. Burlington & Quincy Railway Co.*[1] Just twenty-nine years after the passage of the Fourteenth Amendment, and twenty-four years after the *Slaughterhouse* decision, the Court held that the Fourteenth Amendment "due process" clause incorporated the Fifth Amendment right to be justly compensated if a State (or one of its subdivisions) took your property. In its effect, this case overruled or at least rendered null the 1833 holding, in *Barron v. Baltimore*,[2] that the Fifth Amendment guarantee of compensation for property taken by a government did not apply to the States.

Now if the government takes or desires to take your property, the right to "just compensation" (if it exists at all) is a *substantive* right, just as it is a substantive right in private law to be justly compensated if some other person unlawfully deprives you of your property. It is true that there is a *procedural* right annexed to the substantive right. That is true of every substantive right, if it really is a right. If someone wrongfully takes your property, you have a *procedural* right to sue for compensation. But the basic right is the substantive right not to have your property taken without just compensation.

This substantive right to just compensation for property taken would have fitted with comfort into the "privileges and immunities" clause that was clobbered by the *Slaughterhouse* Court. But clobbered the "privileges and immunities" clause had been. And yet some elementary sense of outrage made it impossible for the Court, in 1897, to let this "taking" go uncompensated. I don't know whether the phrase "substantive due process" had yet been uttered; I rather think it hadn't. But it was not to be borne that the city of Chicago could despoil the railroad of its property without even a theoretical nationally created obligation to pay just compensation. That would be one hell of a way to run the railroads. And so "substantive due process," perhaps still unbaptized under that name, entered the scene as a living thing.

Now when you say those words "substantive due process" over and over, you must see, if you have considered the examples I have given of the difference between substantive law and procedural law or "process," that the phrase is incorrigibly self-contradictory. I tell my students sometimes that it resembles a Zen Buddhist *Koan*, a saying that expresses or asks for the impossible, even the unimaginable, in order to tease or stimulate or press the mind or the spirit into awakening to a transcendent reality, to a transformation of the inmost self. I do not in the least intend to disparage that procedure when it is applied to the spiritual realm, though I am not therein an adept or anything like it, and must look at the matter through a glass darkly, from a great and much obstructed distance. But in all sooth that is not what we are talking about in law. I must repeat the words of my good friend and teacher, the late Jerome Michael, "Law is a practical subject." To generate a powerful and stable field of human-rights law, in a way that will import legitimacy to those who live within it, we need terms that seem to be saying something about human beings. For a thoroughly general system of human rights, we need *general* terms, though we must know that derivation of decisions and rules from those general terms will not exhibit the apodeictic quality of science or mathematics. But we get no aid at all from a term, like "substantive due process," that is simply a contradiction.

The imaginary "substantive due process" clause has nevertheless been used as the flickering imputed source of many substantive rights:

1. The right not to have your property taken without fair compensation (1897), as just seen.

2. The immunity from various forms of governmental activity impinging on economic practices—like the New York law struck down in *Lochner v. New York*,[3] limiting bakers' hours of work to ten a day and sixty a week. Many local, state, and national enactments of this type were successfully challenged. These cases, like the Lochner case itself, were for the most

part soon overruled, and the general line of judicial disapproval of much governmental "economic" regulation passed into disfavor.

3. The right to free speech, extended by liberal analogic and functional reasonings.[4]

4. Freedom of the press, similarly extended.[5]

5. The rights to free exercise of religion,[6] and not to live under rules "respecting" the establishment of religion.[7]

6. The right to teach and to learn foreign languages.[8]

7. The right of parents to send their children to schools other than the public schools (e.g., parochial or military schools)[9]—and a general right of parents to a large share in their children's training.

8. The right to practice contraception.[10]

9. The "fundamental right to marry."[11]

This partial list establishes that, under the phantomic "substantive due process" clause, the Supreme Court has validated many substantive rights. *The "due process" clause is being made to carry the load that would far more naturally have been assigned to the "privileges and immunities" clause of the Fourteenth Amendment, jointly with the two "citizenship" clauses in that Amendment.*

Probably the most important utterance celebrating and in an oblique way explaining this transfer of function (though not under that name) stands in Justice Cardozo's opinion in *Palko v. Connecticut.*[12]

Palko had been convicted, in a state court, of second-degree murder. The *State* appealed this judgment, on the ground that errors of law in the defendant's favor made by the lower state court had resulted in the conviction's being limited to this lower degree of murder, while correct rulings might have cleared the way for a first-degree murder conviction. The Connecticut appellate court agreed with the State, and remanded the case for a second trial, purged of these errors. On this new trial, Palko was convicted of first-degree murder. He applied, in turn, to the Supreme Court of the United States, on the ground that the second trial violated his right to not to be put "twice in jeopardy for the same offense"; he contended that the "due process" clause of the Fourteenth Amendment *incorporated* the Fifth Amendment guarantee against double jeopardy, which otherwise would not have bound the States. Addressing this contention, Cardozo insisted that there was "no such general rule" of total incorporation. He goes on:

> *On the other hand, the due process clause of the Fourteenth Amendment may make it unlawful for a state to abridge by its statutes the freedom of speech which the First Amendment safeguards against encroachment by the Congress, or like the freedom of the press, or the free exercise of religion,* or the right of peaceable assembly, without which speech would be unduly trammeled, or the right of one accused of crime to the benefit of counsel. In these and other situations immunities that are valid as against the federal government by force of the specific pledges of particular Amendments have been found to be *implicit in the concept of ordered liberty,* and thus, through the Fourteenth Amendment, become valid as against the states. . . . The line of division may seem to be wavering and broken if there is a hasty catalogue of the cases on the one side and on the other. Reflection and analysis will induce a different view. There emerges the perception of a rationalizing principle which gives to discrete instances a proper order and coherence. The right to trial by jury and the immunity

from prosecution except as the result of an indictment may have value and importance. Even so, they are not of the very essence of a scheme of ordered liberty. To abolish them *is not to violate a "principle of justice so rooted in the traditions and conscience of our people as to be ranked as fundamental."*

We reach a different plane of social and moral values when we pass to the privileges and immunities that have been taken over from the earlier articles of the federal bill of rights and brought within the Fourteenth Amendment by a process of absorption. These in their origin were effective against the federal government alone. If the Fourteenth Amendment has absorbed them, *the process of absorption has had its source in the belief that neither liberty nor justice would exist if they were sacrificed.* This is true, for illustration, of freedom of thought, and speech. Of that freedom one may say that it is the matrix, the indispensable condition, of nearly every other form of freedom. With rare aberrations a pervasive recognition of that truth can be traced in our history, political and legal. So it has come about that the domain of liberty, withdrawn by the Fourteenth Amendment from encroachment by the states, has been enlarged by latter-day judgments to include liberty of the mind as well as liberty of action.

It is very important to note that this passage, which contains doubtless the most famous and most often-quoted justification for applying First Amendment law against the States, exhibits in just this regard a huge inconsequence of thought. (I raise this because it affords yet another insight into the dangers to clear thought that threaten, when the mind is directed to establishing that the phrase, "due process of law," incorporates *substantive* law.)

The *Palko* case itself concerned *criminal procedure*. Every single example given by Cardozo, on either side of his "line of division," concerns nothing but criminal *procedure*—jury trial, a real trial instead of a sham trial, and so on—except for the shield of free speech and religion. The latter is inserted in such a way as to suggest that the question as to "free speech" or "religious freedom" is much the same sort of question as the one about "right to counsel."

But the questions are not in the same part of the world. It is very clear that "due process of law" refers at a minimum to criminal procedure. The only question is then, "To what aspects and kinds of criminal procedure?" At the least, the original Bill of Rights guarantees, which are largely about criminal procedure, can suggest possibilities to the mind. And that is the use Cardozo makes of them—a very natural use, when one is asking, "What *procedure* is *due*?"

But the question as to "free speech" is not, "What *procedures*, named in the original Bill of Rights, are requisite to 'right *procedure*' under the Fourteenth Amendment 'due process'—that is to say, 'due procedure'—clause?" The question here could hardly be more different: "Does the 'due *process*' clause of the Fourteenth Amendment 'incorporate,' and so make applicable to the States, the *substantive law* of the free speech and religion guarantees?" It has to be added that this is a particularly difficult "incorporation," because the First Amendment addresses its prohibitions *only to Congress*. It is an enormous leap.

It ought to be added that the opinion's approval of the gathering-up of the First Amendment into the Fourteenth's "due process" clause was not strictly relevant to the issue in Palko. But in 1937, the same year, the Court had decided a handful of free-speech cases, in at least one of which this "incorporation" had seemingly been effected.[13] Cardozo's words in Palko became the next thing to definitive grounds for this "incorporation."

(As a matter of fact, the hard rule of the Palko case, as to double jeopardy itself, was expressly overruled in 1969;[14] *Benton v. Maryland*, 395 U.S. 784. I have not had the heart to research the grim question of whether Palko was meanwhile put to death.[15] If he was, perhaps his shade has by now convinced Cardozo's that the right not to be tried twice [or more] for the same alleged offense can be quite "fundamental.")

Now I've gone into all this to illustrate what zigzags and blurrings have to occur when you address yourself to the task of bringing to bear a clause about "due process," which means "due procedure," on matters of substantive law.

I think I ought to say just here that no better illustration ever occurred of the plain truth that "substantive due process" has taken over, though with its own innate feebleness, the function that naturally could and should have been the function of the "privileges and immunities" clause, as its content was foreshadowed by Mr. Justice Washington in *Corfield v. Coryell* (see pp. 49–50, above). Freedom to speak your mind is a precious *substantive right.* Jefferson said, "Knowledge is happiness"; one of the indispensable paths toward that happiness is to communicate with others and to have them free to communicate with you. Who will deny these assertions? Whether we read the Declaration of Independence, or Mr. Justice Washington's *Corfield* opinion, we know that we are committed as a nation to the idea that "the pursuit of happiness" is a basic right of humankind. Isn't that really a better way, a simpler way, a more convincing way to justify the protection of human speech and expression than all these twistings, these misdirections, about "substantive due process"? Doesn't this "pursuit of happiness" entail freedom of religion as well? These "verdurous glooms and winding mossy ways" don't even exemplify *elegantia, juris* or otherwise.

But let that for the moment be. The Cardozo dictum in the Palko case has gone out even beyond free speech and religion, and become an omnibus touchstone. One among the important uses of this sort occurs in the second Justice Harlan's dissent in the *Ullman* case:[16]

> However it is not the particular enumeration of rights in the first eight Amendments which spells out the reach of the Fourteenth Amendment due process, but rather, as was suggested in another context long before the adoption of that Amendment, those concepts which are considered to embrace those rights "which are . . . *fundamental,* which belong . . . to the citizens of all free governments," *Corfield v. Coryell,* for "the purposes [of securing] which men enter into society," *Calder v. Bull.* Due process has not been reduced to any formula; its content cannot be determined by reference to any code. The best that can be said is that through the course of this Court's decisions it has represented the balance which our nation, built upon the postulates of respect for the liberty of the individual, has struck between that liberty and the demands of organized society. If the supplying of content to this Constitutional concept has of necessity been a rational process, it certainly has not been one where judges have felt free to roam where unguided speculation might take them. The balance of which I speak is the balance struck by this country, having regard to what history teaches are the traditions from which it developed as well as the traditions from which it broke. That tradition is a living thing. . . . And inasmuch as this context is one not of words, but of history and pur-

poses, the full scope of the liberty guaranteed by the Due Process Clause cannot be found in or limited by the precise terms of the specific guarantees elsewhere provided in the Constitution. This "liberty" is not a series of isolated points pricked out in terms of the taking of property; the freedom to bear arms; the freedom from unreasonable searches and seizures; and so on. *It is a rational continuum which, broadly speaking, includes a freedom from all substantial arbitrary impositions and purposeless restraints . . . and which also recognizes, what a reasonable and sensitive judgment must, that certain interests require particularly careful scrutiny of the state needs asserted to justify their abridgment.*

Justice Harlan five years later reiterated this position, linking it to Cardozo's *Palko* opinion:

> In my view, the proper constitutional inquiry in this case is whether this Connecticut statute infringes the Due Process Clause of the Fourteenth Amendment because the enactment violates basic values "implicit in the concept of ordered liberty," *Palko v. Connecticut*, 302 U.S. 319, 325. For reasons stated at length in my dissenting opinion in *Poe v. Ullman*, supra, I believe that it does. While the relevant inquiry may be aided by resort to one or more of the provisions of the Bill of Rights, it is not dependent on them or any of their radiations. The Due Process Clause of the Fourteenth Amendment stands, in my opinion, on its own bottom.[17]

Note what has happened here. The Cardozan gloss on "due process," "the scheme of ordered liberty," is functioning as an *independent* and *general criterion*, and not merely as a reason for preferring free speech to some of the other written Bill of Rights guarantees. The phrase has departed from the field of "incorporation" *vel non,* and taken on a general creative force. There is no convincing way to find the substantive right to practice contraception in the specific texts of the original Bill of Rights—the first eight Amendments to the Constitution. In Douglas's opinion for the Court, in the *Griswold* case, an attempt is made to do this by recourse to concepts of "radiations" or "emanations," but that is not likely to seem solid except to those already convinced. It is true that getting convictions under the Connecticut anti-contraception statute might depend on the carrying out of "searches and seizures," some of which might not pass the "probable cause" test of the Fourth Amendment. But that need only mean that convictions might be difficult, as they are in many other cases. There undoubtedly would occur cases in which confession or admission, or very convincing circumstantial evidence, or the chance of a surreptitious third-party (or even a second-party) witness would be of avail. The real reason for the invalidation of the forbidding of contraception by married couples is that to tender to such couples the choice between sexual abstinence on the one hand, and on the other hand having at this time a child they do not want to have, or believe they should not have, is a savage blow to the pursuit of happiness, which is a vouchsafed right in the Declaration of Independence and was recognized as a fundamental "privilege and immunity" of citizenship a century and a half ago in *Corfield v. Coryell.* There could be no better case for exemplifying how much clarity can come from asking, at last, the *right* question.

Why not just stick with "substantive due process," irritating as it is? Because, quite visibly, this non-concept rests on insufficient commitment, and has too little firm meaning (if it has any at all) to beget the kind of confidence, in judges or in others, that ought to underlie the regime of human rights in the country that based and bases its life, and its claims to leadership, on its dedication to human rights.

The whole pattern of "substantive due process" cases exhibits this lack, and its dire results. But the problem is neatly illustrated in the case in which a grandmother faced the necessity of banishing from her house one of her two orphaned grandsons.[18]

I want here to make my point by considering this grandmother in a little more depth.

A Ms. Moore had taken in *two* small grandsons, respectively the sons of *two* different sons of hers who were absent. A zoning ordinance of the City of East Cleveland, by limiting residence in her "zone" to "single families" and by so defining a "single family" as to make it lawful for her to give a home to one of these first cousins but *not to both*, forbade this arrangement. The grandmother was convicted of violating this ordinance. (I still remember the shock that went through an audience in Iceland when I used and stressed this word, *"convicted,"* in stating this case.)

The City brought forward justifications for its law that were "marginal at best," and had "only a tenuous relation" to "overcrowding" and "traffic and parking congestion"—in the words of Mr. Justice Powell, writing the plurality opinion in the Supreme Court. Ms. Moore got to keep on giving a home to both her small grandsons. (My Icelandic audience was relieved, but still a little shocked.)

What would Ms. Moore have had to do to comply with this ordinance? To say merely that she would have had to stop giving family shelter to these two little grandsons is too shallow and hasty a description. Quite crucially, she would have had to *choose* between them, with all that would have entailed, as to them and as to her. She would have had to face consigning one of them to such publicly furnished care as might be available, while depriving the other one of close family association with his own first cousin—the nearest thing he had to a brother or a sister. There might have been available some arrangement for alternating them—say, a month apiece for each of them by turn, at her home and in an orphanage—but it is not clear that such an arrangement would have been possible, and, in any case, it would have had its own steady and recurrent agonies.

Now on the other hand, how much "traffic" and "overcrowding" did these little boys generate? We have to consider this comparatively. If the boys had been brothers, the ordinance would not have forbidden their both living under the same roof with their grandmother. Another grandmother, more abundantly blessed in fact and in law, might have, say, *six* grandchildren, all the children of *one* of her own children; *she* could keep all six of them under the one roof. How much "traffic" and "crowding" is prevented by applying a different rule to these first cousins? Mr. Justice Powell's words, "tenuous" and "marginal," seem restrained.

I will start with the plurality opinion of Mr. Justice Powell; it begins with what looks like an apology:

> Substantive due process has at times been a treacherous field for this Court. There *are* risks when the judicial branch gives enhanced protection to certain substantive liberties

without the guidance of the more specific provisions of the Bill of Rights. As the history of the *Lochner* era demonstrates, there is reason for concern lest the only limits to such judicial intervention become the predilections of those who happen at the time to be Members of this Court. That history counsels caution and restraint. But it does not counsel abandonment, nor does it require what the city urges here: cutting off any protection of family rights at the first convenient, if arbitrary boundary—the boundary of the nuclear family.

I am irresistibly reminded here of a reviewer's criticism of an actor appearing in *Hamlet*: "He played the King as though he were afraid somebody else might be about to play the ace." But Justice Powell is not to be faulted for this. "Substantive due process" is thin ice; you walk warily, and listen for cracks.

(As to the quotation about the King in *Hamlet*, I can't now put my hand on it. All I know is that I didn't make it up. How I wish I had!)

Let's look next at Mr. Justice White's *dissenting* opinion:

I cannot believe that the interest in residing with more than one set of grandchildren is one that calls for any kind of heightened protection under the Due Process Clause. To say that one has a personal right to live with all, rather than some, of one's grandchildren and that this right is implicit in ordered liberty is, as my Brother Stewart says, "to extend the limited substantive contours of the Due Process Clause beyond recognition." The present claim is hardly one of which it could be said that "neither liberty nor justice would exist if [it] were sacrificed."

Mr. Justice Powell would apparently construe the Due Process Clause to protect from all but quite important state regulatory interests any right or privilege that in his estimate is deeply rooted in the country's traditions. For me, this suggests a far too expansive character for this Court and a far less meaningful and less confining guiding principle than Mr. Justice Stewart would use for serious substantive due process review. What the deeply rooted traditions of the country are is arguable; which of them deserve the protection of the Due Process Clause is even more debatable. The suggested view would broaden enormously the horizons of the Clause; and, if the interest involved here is any measure of what the States would be forbidden to regulate, the courts would be substantively weighing and very likely invalidating a wide range of measures that Congress and State legislatures think appropriate to respond to a changing economic and social order.

These words rest on a hardly hidden major premise of virtually boundless *negative* judicial discretion as to the protection of human rights. What they say is, "I really think this is going rather too far, it will be a means of letting in upon us a flood of litigation." Such words should be impossible to write (or so I should hope) against any other background than that of perceived or felt fundamental weakness in the concept of "substantive due process." Justice White obviously thinks of that concept as one that may perhaps, now and then, justify a little protection of unnamed rights, but not very much—a concept easily malleable, not to solid distinctions of law, but to intuitive fears of judicial inconvenience. The passage is a perfect illustration of what you can lose when you rely on a highly vulnerable and totally puzzling general theory—such as "substantive due process."

I have stressed the intellectual hopelessness of "substantive due process." This pair of opinions—Powell's and White's— illustrates very well another baneful function of that non-concept. These opinions could prick out the start of a graph of the *feeble force* of this hapless concept, of the conviction and confidence it fails to beget. Mr. Justice Powell deals with it warily, as though it were about to fade away. Mr. Justice White treats it as of no force, properly speaking, at all.

Now that's no way for judges in a country that calls itself free to approach the problem whether a grandmother must turn one of her small grandsons out because somebody down at City Hall thinks, without any shown plausibility, that their both staying with her will create a parking problem and possible overcrowding.

What would happen if we finally threw the switch that would connect us with one of the most comprehensive and authoritative of our great commitments—"the right . . . to the pursuit of happiness?" A judge brought up in *that* tradition would come into court hardly able to contain his indignation that any governmental unit had dared try such a thing. I cannot think that Mr. Justice White would have felt differently. Each of the judges would have asked himself: (1) Is this a heart-crushing blow to the pursuit of happiness? and (2) Are the proffered justifications good enough to justify so heavy a blow? The answers are obvious. *This is what happens when you ask the right questions.*

There is nothing that should be of more anxious and perpetual concern to legal work, including above all the work of judgment, than "Are we asking the right questions?" And we will not be asking the right questions until we swear off "substantive due process" cold turkey and ask the questions authorized by our birthright commitments to human rights, and above all to the right to the "pursuit of happiness," as brought down to us by the Ninth Amendment, and by the Lincolnian "new birth of freedom," that ought to have been found, and ought still to be found, in the "citizenship" and "privileges and immunities" clauses of the Fourteenth Amendment.

Necessity, it is said, is the mother of invention. Sometimes the necessity is so pressing that it gives birth to an invention that doesn't work very well. That is how we got "substantive due process." It was unthinkable that in a supposedly free country the component States could at their own will suppress freedom of speech and religion, forbid contraception for no secular end, make a grandmother throw out one of her two little grandsons, impose unmeetable conditions on the right to marry, forbid people to learn a foreign language, and so on. As these and other examples show, "substantive due process" is an invention that now and then works a little bit in practice, but *does not work* intellectually. It has had perhaps a good transitional function, like the wood-frame support of an arch before you put the keystone in.

## Chapter 4

# JUDICIAL
# REVIEW AND
# MAJORITARIANISM

"The majority rules."

But the concept of "majority" is, at one and the same time, both essential and highly elusive. A majority of whom or what? How does or can one determine the existence of a majority?

In a democracy like ours, a stable and resolute national majority, if fairly evenly distributed throughout the country, can usually find a way to have its way. That is something like all the pure "democracy" that any country has or can have, perhaps all a country can bear and not oscillate into turbulence.

If what this perdurable and tenacious majority wants is the following of some policy not touching human-rights issues, its way to victory is relatively easy—though by no means always and absolutely so. If there arises instead a genuine issue of human rights under the Constitution, there may and often does arise the problem of judicial review.

Judicial review is not even arguably a "usurpation." It has as sure a warrant to existence under our Constitution and laws as does the power of the President (even in his second, lame-duck term) to name ambassadors, who must be confirmed by the population-skewed Senate. (Not just sort of skewed, but very heavily—one might say grotesquely—skewed.) I shall back up this claim a little later on. But for now let me just point out that this legitimacy of judicial review, like the legitimacy of the presidential power to nominate ambassadors, is ultimately subject to the will of a sufficiently strong and stable majority. Constitutional amendment could end either of these practices. It is vitally important, too, that neither of them is "counter-majoritarian" in its inception. Each became part of the Constitution (like everything else in the Constitution) by such "majoritarian" validation as was available in 1787–89. Judicial review of *State* actions for their *national* constitutionality is distinctly commanded by Article VI of the Constitution. Judicial review of Acts of Congress for their validity is unmistakably commanded by an Act of Congress that is itself still in full effect (see pp. 120–121 below) and its legitimacy is clearly assumed in many other acts of Congress. We have judicial review, after all, because the people of the whole country have not exhibited *in action* any desire to abolish it. It has been, by clear implication at the very least and sometimes by something stronger, affirmatively approved and facilitated by Congress. This is because nothing like a steady majority of the people really disapproves of "judicial review" as a whole and in principle, but only of some of the outcomes of judicial review. Try to find somebody who thinks the "contraception" case was forbiddenly "anti-majoritarian" and who has the same view as to the application to the States,[1] through the dubious use of the Fourteenth Amendment, of the doctrine that private property may not be taken by a State for public use without just compensation, whatever a "majority" in that State may want. Opposition to judicial review is a sometime thing—like "strict construction" of the powers of Congress.

How purely "majoritarian" are our other government institutions, in theory or in practice?

On the national constitutional level, the answer has to be "not obsessively so." Let us look over the ways in which the people who form our highest policies are to be chosen. There is the small fact that the presidential electoral system makes it clearly possible (though, as time has shown, not likely) that a President may be elected by the votes of a minority of the voters—by fewer popular votes than his nearest competitor. (I believe this has happened in about one case out of twenty.)

Under the Twelfth Amendment, if there is no majority of electors (a thing that might easily occur), the choice of one among the *three* highest candidates (in electoral votes) goes into the House of Representatives. In the vote there, *each State has one vote.* There can here be no thought of "popular majority," as essential to legitimacy, when Alaska and California have the same voting strength. Since, moreover, it takes *twenty-six States*—each casting *one vote*—("a majority of the whole number of States") to select a President in the House, and since Alaska and California each cast *one* vote, and since any State with an even number of Congressmen may be tied, or by some other distribution fail to create a majority within itself for any candidate, and so be unable to cast a vote, it may be very difficult to muster these twenty-six votes. 25–12–13 would not do it; 23–10–8 would not do it. Not even 25–25 would do it. Since the twenty-five may contain a total population much greater or much smaller than that of either the twelve or the thirteen or both together (58% of the American people live in nine states), that might mean that a choice would be impossible, though a popular majority choice existed. Very likely, there would be a "deal," but each low-population State would negotiate with just the same strength as the highest-population State—and one Congressman whose vote might change the vote of a State would negotiate with a strength all but entirely unrelated to numbers of people. A result that reflects the wishes of a majority of the American people, however that may be ascertained, is one possibility, but it is far from a certainty or even a very strong likelihood.

If no result is reached in the House of Representatives, by a "deal" or otherwise, nobody is elected President, and then the person elected Vice President takes over the Presidency. Since the Constitution calls for a vote in the Senate between the two vice-presidential candidates with the highest electoral votes, and since the Senate chooses by a general vote, a tie is unlikely. But if it occurs it would necessarily have to be resolved by the Vice President (outgoing, though he may be a just-defeated lame duck). Remember again that the Senate does not represent the American people *per capita* with even approximate equality. A strong "majority" in the Senate need not express the desires of a majority of the whole people. A bare majority in the Senate may easily be representative of a decided minority of the people. A tie in the Senate does not imply a tie in popular desire.

Now that's the way the President may be chosen. If the spread of votes is fairly even geographically, and if the popular majority is fairly large, *and if no strong third candidate draws* enough strength in a few States to capture their electoral votes, the system works tolerably well. But this tolerable working is not something that inheres in the system as set up in the Constitution. It has been attained only by the growing up of extra-constitutional devices that strongly tend toward drastically narrowing down the number of candidates who can be taken seriously. If there are only two candidates then it is near certain that one of them will get an electoral majority. The system does not work to secure the election as President of the person a majority of the people want as their first choice, for the good reason that, since George Washington, no such person normally, if ever, has existed. It is a system that conduces to a tolerable compromise.

The person who may be put in the presidential office by this process, flawed as it is from the pure majoritarian point of view, appoints all the principal officers of the United States, guides and sets our foreign policy, makes through appointees immeasurable administrative decisions affecting millions of people, holds the commandership-in-chief of the armed forces, and exercises the awesome power of the veto of Congressional actions, including statutes (a power, by the way, very problematic from the majoritarian point of view). What is the "majority" to be taken to want, when the Houses of Congress pass a bill, then the President vetoes it, and the override vote *just barely* falls short of two thirds in one house? As I believe I have demonstrated above, the person who has this veto power is not selected by a single popular-majority vote, nor by processes that guarantee its equivalence. In his second term of four years, the President need not think of a *future* election.

It is not my purpose here to express disapproval of all this. Straight-out popular election would have its own grave problems; it has been often considered and never in the final result adopted even by the Congress that would have to propose the necessary constitutional amendment. My purpose is a different one—to show that, as to choice of the President, our system, as originally set up and as it now stands, is not anything like committed to pure majoritarian principle.

The limitation of the President to two terms, like all "term limits" so-called, is radically anti-majoritarian, even "undemocratic." No matter how strong the popular desire may be, no matter what special circumstances produce this desire, the second-term President is ineligible to reelection.

How about the procedures for choosing people to serve in Congress? One needn't say much about the Senate! But one ought to think a lot about it. The population ratio between California and Alaska is about sixty-five to one, yet each of these States sends two Senators, and this huge disparity is guaranteed even against constitutional amendment, unless *Alaska* consents (see Article V). The naked constitutional theory is, then, that when it comes to the Senate, States with widely different populations are to have the same representation in that upper House, even though almost all the States and nearly all the people might agree that this apportionment of Senatorial power ought to be changed. How "majoritarian" is that?

Nor is it to the point that the Senate's function in passing laws can be looked on as "merely" negative. (This might equally be said of the more nearly "majoritarian" House of Representatives.) The power to refuse passage is the power to influence and sometimes to dictate content. It is also the power to refuse to repeal any law now in force.

This Senate, constituted without any attention at all to proportion of population, or to any "majoritarian" theory, has the power to confirm or deny confirmation to presidential appointments to federal offices, including ambassadorships and judgeships, and to *refuse* ratification to treaties by *one third plus one* of its membership. A treaty disfavored by that many Senators may be strongly favored by a majority of the American people. On the other hand, two-thirds of the Senate may (though it is not very likely) represent less than a majority of the American people, since 58% of the people live in nine states, sending eighteen Senators.

The House of Representatives, the "democratic" branch, is elected by *districts*. Since every State must under Article I have an integral number of Congressmen of its own, there is some disproportion between States in the number of persons represented by Congressman—because some States have populations just large enough to have, say, three Congressmen, and some States have almost but not quite enough to get four. You can check this out in any World Almanac. Perhaps these, and similar disparities, are not very serious. What is serious is the possibility, one that exists in any geographical-district system, that a majority of the House may have had the votes of a minority of the national aggregate of voters. This was not far from happening in 1994; what was hailed as a Republican congressional "landslide" was actually a fairly close-run thing in popular vote, nationwide, as between the two parties. Such a thing's not happening depends on the near-even geographical distribution of party-vote. More districts like the New

York City district of Charles Rangel could easily swamp, in aggregate popular vote, five or six districts where candidates of the opposite party ran ahead in close elections.

I am not against this either. On balance of all factors, I think the district system very likely works better, for us, than proportional representation would; in any case our Constitution would make it just about impossible to institute proportional representation.

But the entrance on the national scene of even one strong third party, let alone more than one, can change things. This is dramatically shown in the last election Margaret Thatcher won in Britain. She governed, both before and after that election, more or less in the tone and style of Napoleon I. But she had won only 43% of the popular vote. That election shows that third parties, which benevolent folk often hail as "giving the people a wider choice," may end up giving those people whose choice of policies is more or less alike, the choice of putting in power the crowd they like least of the three. Isn't this what probably happened in Lady Thatcher's 43% "triumph?"

Now I am not attacking the national government as "undemocratic." I am simply showing that it is *not* majoritarian in strict theory or practice. It balances doctrinaire "majoritarianism" with other values and devices. (The only one of these devices I cannot approve of or understand is the one that comes into play when and if nobody gets a majority of the presidential electoral votes. To set up for such a case a "one-state-one-vote" rule in the House of Representatives radically changes the constituency base of the original group of "electors" and adopts the "Senatorial" model of equal votes for each State. I can't think why this was considered a good change, particularly when the first electoral ratio to population might have been roughly replicated by giving the choice to a joint session of the House and the Senate with each member having one vote, thus taking a "second opinion" from a new Congress constituted on the same mixed basis as the original Presidential electors, and incidentally eliminating the problems that can arise if a State's delegation is tied up and so unable to vote at all.)

I've devoted this much analysis to the national government because that, for a reason I'll shortly give, seems to me to be the only one that matters, the only one whose quasi-"majoritarianism" really needs to be brought into view. But I think one can validly though summarily say that all the States exhibit in one way or another this falling from the dubious grace of doctrinaire majoritarianism, yet, like the national government, have that mediated and sometimes slow response to stable and persistent popular will that is probably the best kind of "democracy." The alternative is government by very frequent single-issue plebiscite; I have elsewhere explored what I believe to be the fatal flaws in one fairly recent and relatively modest proposal for national legislation by referendum.[2]

Why have I said that anything like a real clash with majoritarianism does not exist in the case of the collision of state laws and other local actions with *nationally* established human rights? I would think that the question answers itself in Article VI: "This Constitution, and the Laws of the United States which shall be made in Pursuance thereof; and all Treaties made, or which shall be made, under the Authority of the

United States, shall be the supreme Law of the Land; and the Judges in every state shall be bound thereby, any Thing in the Constitution or Laws of any State to the Contrary notwithstanding."

Since the great majority of cases that strike down state laws, in first instance or on final appeal, in the interest of human rights, rest on claimed *national* rights, and since the action rests on the interpretation of *national* law by *national* judicial officers, commissioned for this work by the *national* government, and since, though Article VI appears to answer this "majoritarian" objection as to state law cases, it continues to be urged as to them, one might say a bit more.

The uniform interpretation of national human-rights law, *as of all national law*, is a prime national function, guarding our practical and moral unity as a nation. Without such interpretation the national law of human rights is at the mercy of the States, one by one. No one would think of contending that a valid Act of Congress or a treaty must be interpreted and applied with a generous measure of deference to "majority" sentiment in one or more States. I can't think why this should not be true as to human-rights positions. Again, one wonders about the result of the Civil War. This "majoritarian" stuff, treating state majorities as a factor for weakening national law, is just "nullification" in clumsily stitched sheep's clothing.

Now so far I've dealt only with the principal power-expressions of national and state governments and with the organs that are given responsibility for these. But another point needs making, on this "majoritarian" matter: Many claimed infractions of national human rights occur through the actions of delegees or sub-delegees or sub-sub-delegees of national *or* state power.

There are indefinitely many such cases. A Secretary of State decides to withhold a passport. A police chief decides how to interrogate a suspect, and a state judge upholds him. A local zoning board votes to keep a grandmother from taking in more than one of her grandchildren to live with her, unless they are all offspring of the same one of her children. A mother claims that her retarded, involuntarily committed son suffered deprivation of constitutional rights when officials of a state institution gave him inadequate protection against injury. The Board of Regents of a state university does not rehire a teacher, allegedly because of things he has said.

In all such cases, the issue of "majoritarianism" is fictive, because *neither* a national *nor* a state "majority" is in any showable way implicated—unless you mean something like "the majority of the zoning board," or the one to zero "majority" of the police chief.

(None of this is said in derogation of "delegation." The non-rule that a delegated power may not be delegated is absolutely impossible of application to any complicated enterprise, including government. That is the way most decisions have to be made. But the delegation to a zoning board of the decision whether the rule in the grandmother case is a good one on *local* considerations [see above] cannot *be held to foreclose from fullest inquiry the question whether such a rule violates a national constitutional human right or any other national law.* And the concept of majoritarianism, proffered as a ground for such deference, is the substitution of fiction for fact.)

There is only one authority that even faintly arguably expresses the will of a national majority on a question of *national* rights—that is, the Congress, by the passage (and including either the signature of the President or passage over his veto) of a national law. That is the closest thing to the expression of the national majority will and understanding that we have. As I have shown, it has both major and minor imperfections. It also may have a rather short half-life, if viewed non-fictively, because, first, anybody who knows anything about Congress knows that repeal is not something that rather automatically occurs as soon as only 45% of the people now are of the same mind as they were, and secondly, because the President, perhaps in his second "lame duck" term, may veto the repeal, and thereby subject repeal to a ⅔ + ⅔ double bottleneck with no possibility that he will ever face the voters. All this gets rather fanciful, but that is because the idea of "majoritarianism" is itself rather fanciful. And (one cannot too often repeat) let us not lose sight of its entire unsuitability when applied to the States (against which most human-rights complaints are made) and to subordinate officials, both national and state.

The only thing not quite meaningless, as an application of the idea of majoritarianism to *nationally vouchsafed* human rights, would be the committing of such decisions to formal actions of *Congress*. But that is hardly even imaginable. Congress has neither time nor resources for going into a question about the zoning law as applied in East Cleveland, or the constitutional fairness of the treatment accorded to a retarded institutional inmate. Congress is a non-starter here. The alternative would be an elaborate administrative network with investigative and adjudicative power to move in and deal with this legion of unforeseeably occurring cases, trying the facts and deciding the law. Why would anybody think that to be a better way than using the judges to do this job of judging? The *individuation* of law, including constitutional law, is the business of judges.

Until the question can be answered, maybe we should, as it were, tentatively be thankful that we *have* the judges, and that their work in this regard is of well-attested legitimacy, both as to state law and practices and as to national law and practices, when either of these confronts a national human-rights claim.

As to the States, ponder Article VI yet again: It says that whatever the Constitution (as amended) may be held to provide is part of "the supreme Law of the Land; and the Judges in every State shall be bound thereby . . ."

Now I don't know how you'd get around that. The only way is to gloss the words *"Judges in every State"* as meaning "the state judiciaries." But note that (aside from the absurdity of a Constitution that would oblige state judges but not federal judges to obey it) it ignores the listing of the Constitution as a component in "the supreme Law of the Land." How could federal judges fail to apply that law, part of the "supreme Law," to state actions? And federal judges *do* sit "in" the States.

What about Congressional actions? Here the argument is slightly more complicated, though I think not of doubtful outcome. The Supremacy clause of Article VI establishes that the Constitution is *law,* inviolable in all courts. The remaining question is whether it has the status of a *superior* law, as against the two other kinds of "supreme Law of the Land"—Acts of Congress and treaties. To establish that it does, you have to read the Constitution itself. It speaks with unmistakable authority. Article I, Section 9, categorically forbids the passage by Congress of *ex post facto* laws and bills of attainder. The First Amendment rests on the same assumption: "Congress shall make no law . . ." But one need not stop there. If you start reading Article I, you find that the composition of Congress, and the qualifications for voting in congressional elections, are set out with the voice of authority; no action by a body not constituted in this way is even to be looked on as taken by "Congress." The intervals between elections for the House and the Senate are prescribed (contrasting with the British conception of an omnipotent Parliament that, regardless of prior agreement or understanding, could and did change the corresponding interval from three years to seven, in the famous Septennial Act of Queen Anne's day). Congress is peremptorily forbidden to lay a tax or duty on articles exported from any State. But why go on with this? If ever a document spoke with the claim, literally irresistibly and repeatedly implied, of being a law that is to govern and control another kind of law, our whole Constitution speaks that way. Of course this applies *a fortiori* to the actions of other federal officials.

The pure constitutional case for judicial review of the constitutionality of state and federal laws and other governmental acts of power seems clear. When somebody at a cocktail party says that such review is not mandated or contemplated by the Constitution, I tell them to take two aspirin and get a good night's sleep. One more piece of evidence might make that sleep more tranquil—Section 25 of the Judiciary Act of 1789, passed by the first Congress, in which sat a good many people who had been at the Constitutional Convention just two years before:

> That a final judgment or decree in any suit, in the highest court of law or equity of a State in which a decision in the suit could be had, where is drawn in question the validity of a treaty or statute of, or an authority exercised under the

United States, and the decision is against their validity; or where is drawn in question the validity of a statute, or an authority exercised under any state, on the ground of their being repugnant to the Constitution, treaties or laws of the United States, and the decision is in favor of such their validity, or where is drawn in question the construction of any clause of the Constitution, or of a treaty, or statute of, or commission held under the United States, and the decision is against the title, right, privilege or exemption specially set up or claimed by either party, under such clause of the said Constitution, treaty, statute or commission, may be reexamined and reversed or affirmed in the Supreme Court of the United States upon a writ of error. [But] no other error shall be assigned or regarded as a ground of reversal in any such case aforesaid, than such as appears on the face of the record, and immediately respects the beforementioned questions of validity or construction of the said Constitution, treaties, statutes, commissions, or authorities in dispute.

This language names certain kinds of cases which are expected to come up, how frequently no one could have guessed, in the state courts, and to have been decided there in certain ways. It then confers appellate jurisdiction on the Supreme Court of the United States, in certain of these decided state cases.

There are three classes of cases named, somewhat simplified:

(1) One in which the state court has finally decided *against* the validity of a statute passed by Congress (such decisions could only be on the ground of the repugnance of the Act of Congress to the Constitution).

(2) One in which the state court has finally decided *in favor* of the validity of a *state statute* as against the claim that it is repugnant to the national Constitution or laws.

(3) One in which a claim of right has been based in the national Constitution and laws, and the state court decision has been *against* the party claiming such national right.

In all three cases, the decision of the state court denying the federal claim (including a federal constitutional claim) is to be taken up by the national Supreme Court as a court of appeal, *and reversed or affirmed.*

The first thing to notice about this statute is that it simply *assumes* that such cases, turning on the validity of federal constitutional claims, will be an expectable part of state judicial business. Remember that this Act was passed in 1789 and signed by George Washington. This is very persuasive evidence of the "original understanding;" they didn't feel any need to *grant* state courts jurisdiction over such cases; the occurrence of such cases was simply assumed, as a part of the normal judicial work of all courts. You must note that (except for a brief interval) there did not exist, until 1875, any lower federal courts with *general* jurisdiction over cases "arising under" the national Constitution and laws. It resulted that such cases could and would be brought in the state courts, and this section's provision for appeal to the Supreme Court was to be, until after the Civil War, the only sure guard for the national interest in the prevalence of national law.

Back to Section 25 of the 1789 Act: One crucial thing is yet to be added. As to all three of the categories of cases set out as subject to Supreme Court review, *each such case is to be "re-examined and reversed or affirmed"* by that Court. *Now what does it mean to affirm a case that has held an Act of Congress invalid? Does it not mean to approve of and to confirm the state court's holding that the Act is invalid? This statute of 1789 therefore contains a congressional direction that the Supreme Court, as a court of appeal, take up and re-examine a case that has held an Act of Congress to be invalid, and affirm that holding if the Supreme Court thinks it correct.*

I am spelling this all out because it is one of the "Tested Sentences That Sell," in the Two Hundred Years War about "judicial review," that Congress has not even acquiesced in the Court's claims to the power to invalidate Acts of Congress. How can people go on saying that? Here, in an Act of Congress passed in 1789, and signed into law by George Washington, Congress goes further than merely acquiescing; it directs the Court to perform this function, where it is, as a court of law, free to reverse, or to *affirm* if convinced that validation of the Act of Congress is required. That 1789 Act, George Washington's signature and all, is as "majoritarian" as you can get. It also sets up a kind of paradox. In order to hold this Act, the 1789 act, not binding on itself in this particular, the Court would have had to hold this section of the 1789 Act of Congress unconstitutional.

This particular "majoritarian" action has not been receded from. This Act of 1789 has been codified over and over again, and modified only in ways completely consistent with its main message. Matthew Arnold encountered, in a Celtic epic poem, a warrior of whom it was said, "He went forth to battle, but he always fell." There has been fulmination and agitation in Congress, through the decades, against judicial review. But Congress, *as Congress*, acts only through the passage of bills, orders, resolutions, and votes. And Congress in two hundred years has never passed any law, or any "Bill, Order, Resolution or Vote," impairing the force of this direction to *reverse or affirm.* Instead, Congress has often facilitated the performance of this function. Judicial review is as lawful and as thoroughly legitimated as anything in the government of the United States. It is one with apple pie.

I think it is well that this should be so. To the reasons I gave thirty-five years ago, in my first book on constitutional law, I would add another. An active federal judiciary is the most hopeful bulwark for human rights in the United States. Or, one may fear in hours of dark thought, the least hopeless—but even that is something.

*If human rights are to be kept ever-refreshed, seeing to this must be the business of somebody.* The attainment and keeping of this good requires vigilance and effort. Every articulated set of values in government *must have its executors.*[3]

The federal judiciary is very, very far from perfect for this purpose. But at last we have to face the question, "Who is better?"

This is not a new question; the most decided early answer to it was given by Madison in Congress as he argued for the adoption of the Bill of Rights, in 1789:

> If they are incorporated into the Constitution, independent tribunals of justice will consider themselves in a peculiar manner the guardians of those rights; They will be an impenetrable bulwark against every assumption of power in the Legislative or the Executive; They will be naturally *led* to resist every encroachment upon rights expressly stipulated for in the Constitution . . .[4]

It is true that Madison, with Jefferson, came to have deep disagreements with some actions of the federal judiciary, particularly in the case of the Circuit Judges who upheld the Alien and Sedition Acts, but that disagreement was based on those judges' not being *vigorous enough* in protecting human rights by the judicial power. Jefferson was dissatisfied, in that controversy, with the federal judges' not having been sufficiently "activist," not "anti-majoritarian" enough. (The Alien and Sedition law was, after all, an Act of Congress, the nearest thing to an embodiment of a national majority.)

I am not out to eulogize our federal judges one by one. No indeed. But as an organized corps, the federal judiciary has at least a *capacity* for serving the cause of human rights, in time to come, that seems to me the most hopeful—or, perhaps, the least hopeless. There is given a way; whether the will can grow time alone must tell—from time to time. Of what *other* corps, now in existence or foreseeably likely to come into existence, is even this much true? Can anything better be said, *mutatis mutandis*, of Congress or the Presidency?

Particular suitors can approach a *court* with a claim of right that must be heard, and expect to hear *reasons* for the disposition made of the claim. These reasons are openly given, and those having any general interest are normally published; this gives full scope to criticism, and at the same time may augment the understanding of other judges working the same decisional process. Human-rights claims are made *in the name of the law*, as the outcome of *reasoning from commitment*; judges are practiced in this kind of reasoning, and some of them are expert at it.

What corps of persons, institutionally capable of giving actual life to human rights, has these indispensable characteristics, even though the realization of these characteristics to their fullest is far from universal? An elaborate *administrative* framework, charged with the same responsibilities? Whereof would we form such a corps, or find the will to do so? Would not the people who formed that corps, at their best, simply resemble judges?

Our history has provided us with such a corps. The price we pay for it is life tenure, which in practice means an average of say fifteen to twenty years. (I haven't done the simple arithmetic on this lately; when I wrote my earlier book on judicial review, in 1959, the average term of all the Supreme Court justices since the Civil War was about thirteen years.) In any case it is a price that Madison knew all about when he made the statement I have quoted above; it is the price successive Congresses have been willing to pay; it is the price of immunity from pressure, necessary as a condition to steadfast commitment to human rights—though not, alas, always a sufficient one.

I would conclude now, as Madison did over two centuries ago, that the commitment of judges to this (among other) work is a good deal. Not a perfect one. But what would be a perfect deal?

I would make one final point about this. It is a good deal even as to the invalidation of Acts of Congress, the only actions even close to "majoritarian" on the national level—on the same level, that is to say, as nationally ordained human rights. But it is a deal indispensably necessary in a nation having the structure of ours, with fifty local authorities, the States, competent to handle virtually any subject matter unless national law conflicts. There has to be some corps of authorities acting for the national interest as to any claimed violation of any kind, by the States, of nationally established human rights, just as there is in regard to claimed violations of any other national law. Without that, something we call "Our Federalism" (however reverentially capitalized) can be the Catch-22 of human-rights guarantees virtually anywhere in our national territory.

If you doubt the concrete realism of this, read a lot of cases, in the Reports, of what the States have tried to do, and been kept from doing by the federal courts.

Let us thankfully use these judges for what could be—and in some cases already is—their highest function: the making good of our claims, before the world, of being a country wherein governments are restrained from acting in ways destructive to liberty and obstructive to the pursuit of happiness. That is exactly what we promised on the first day of our nationhood. If the ongoing fulfillment of that promise cannot be kept in process by a corps of judges, it can't be accomplished at all, at least in our political system as it stands and will in enormous likelihood continue to stand. The national Congress is not so structured as to be up to the vigorous and vigilant detail work, or to the steadfastness of vision that is required. As to the States, the prospect for *moral* nationhood would be not merely bleak but absolutely hopeless.

Perhaps a nation is fated to play out again and again the same plot. Today we seem to be fighting the Civil War all over again. The myth of state sovereignty ought to have been seen to be obsolete when the first State was admitted to the Union out of territory already belonging to the nation. (Kentucky,

I make it, in 1792, over two hundred years ago.) Wisconsin, among about thirty-three other states, never had any arguable sovereignty to give up. Indeed, from 1788 on, state "sovereignty" was a paradoxical puzzle, for the States were subjected to the supremacy of national law by the Constitution (which, unlike the Articles of Confederation, contains no reservation of their "sovereignty"). They were from the beginning denied powers pertaining to "sovereignty"—coining money, making treaties, engaging in war except in case of imminent danger that would not admit delay. The core power of "sovereignty"—stating what shall be the "supreme Law of the Land"—was denied them by Article VI of the Constitution of 1788. It's been downhill for state "sovereignty" ever since. In the Fourteenth Amendment, each State was stripped of the power to say who should be its citizens, and in later Amendments, who among these citizens were not to be denied the right to vote in state elections. I put it to you that nobody reading the Constitution and all its Amendments would think they were dealing with "sovereign" States. That's just Civil War talk, though we're still hearing it a hundred and thirty years after the end of that war.

And we need to be aware of it in this context. If national judicial review of state actions ceased to occur, there would be no security for any human rights to which the nation, as a nation, is committed. Justice Oliver Wendell Holmes, Jr., and Justice Joseph Story clearly saw that the only security for the law of the Union was in the national judicial power to review state actions. This is still true, and always will be true, unless the world utterly changes. Absent such review, the *obligatory* law of human rights in general would be the law of the State or States least oriented, for the time being, toward the defense of human rights.

Why don't we face reality? We actually have only one corps of people—the federal judges—who have *in principle* the job of policing human rights in the name of national political morality, and who are so organized as to be able to do this work. The work of the federal judges in this regard sometimes does not have a quality pleasing to someone devoted to the ideal of a comprehensive regime of human rights. But at least there is hope of it.

## Chapter 5

# THE CONSTITUTIONAL JUSTICE OF LIVELIHOOD

You will not be surprised when I tell you that I think the place to start on this is the Declaration of Independence. The Declaration indelibly identifies the rights to life, liberty, and the pursuit of happiness as the inalienable endowment of humankind, and tells us that the quintessential purpose of government is to "secure these rights," and so (as the basic condition of its tenure), to "effect," so far as may be, the safety and the happiness of its people.

Well, many do die, quickly sometimes, sometimes more slowly, of poverty. "Liberty" is pervasively deadened by poverty into a dumb simulacrum, clean-shorn of "the *blessings* of liberty." But the "right to the pursuit of happiness" is enough to go on with. As a *right*, and not as a mere mocking truism (like a slave's "right" to choose whether his "happiness" will be better served by picking cotton all day "in the summertime, when the living is easy," or by being whipped), the right to the pursuit of happiness is the right to be in a situation where that pursuit has some reasonable and continually refreshed chance of moving toward its goal. The duty of government to *secure* this right is a duty to *act* affirmatively, just as the duty to effect the safety of the people is a duty so to act. (I have said enough elsewhere of the carrying-over of such claims into constitutional law, in the strictest sense, by the Ninth Amendment rule of construction—though it is my view that the Declaration itself is sufficient.)

There is more to be said as to the textual basis for a *constitutional* "justice of livelihood." Let us go to the Preamble to the Constitution, and to an echoing of the preamble in Article I, Section 8. The Preamble declares that a purpose of the Constitution is to "promote the general Welfare." Then, in a phrasal echo that can hardly be accidental, means are bestowed on Congress to tax and spend "for the . . . general Welfare." Do not these twinned phrases pick up and carry forward the very themes of the pursuit of happiness and of the duty of government to aim at maximizing happiness, that are found in the Declaration? And does not the possession of the *power* to seek and to support the general welfare generate a resulting *duty* to do these very things—even without the Declaration, strongly corroboratory though that document be?

There will always be some vagueness about the boundaries of the concept "general welfare." But our American generation is in the happy or unhappy position of not having to worry about these peripheral and penumbral problems. It is a clarifying metaphor, pointing to ugly truth, to say that our country contains two countries—a country wherein everybody has plenty of good food to eat, and a country wherein nutrition is a bad problem and getting worse. In one country, infant mortality, the death of babies, is going down; in the other country it is going up. A house thus divided against itself is not a penumbral case on the general-welfare question. It is a classic case—I ought better to say *the* classic case—of welfare diffused not *generally* but instead *partially*—with, as we all know, scandalously strong streaks of racism and sexism in that partiality.

The possession of a decent material basis for life is an indispensable condition, for almost all people at all times, to the pursuit of happiness. The lack of this basis—the lack we call "poverty"—is overwhelmingly, in the whole human world, the commonest, the grimmest, the stubbornest obstacle we know to the pursuit of happiness. I have suggested that poverty may be the leading cause of death; it is pretty certain that it is the leading cause, at least among material causes, of despair in life. Of course some few people, through extraordinary talent or rabbit's foot luck (and talent is itself a gift of luck), do clamber over the obstacle. But the right to the pursuit of happiness is going to be, for all but a small minority of those in poverty, the pale sardonically grinning ghost of a right.

I go on now to the *affirmative constitutional duty* of Congress diligently to devise and prudently to apply the means necessary to ensure, humanly speaking, a decent livelihood for all.

We have, to be sure, tended to conceive of constitutional human-rights law as a set of limitations on governmental power. This concept contains much health, but not the whole truth. A serious thirst for human rights, and so for human-rights law, cannot be slaked with no more than a canon of "thou shalt not's." Sins against human rights are not only those of commission, but those of omission as well. Other nations seem to have gotten ahead of us in explicit and detailed recognition of this; herein the papacy has outstripped the United States of America. We started the conversation about human rights, but we seem reluctant to carry it forward.

Since we are talking about human rights as a part of our own constitutional law, it might be useful to ask whether affirmative duties are exotic in that law. We closely study the *empowerments* of the national government, the *distributions* of power within it, and the *limitations* that lie upon it, devoting little attention to the Constitution as a source of affirmative obligation to act, sometimes on a very grand scale.

If we start at the beginning, we read no further than Article I, Section 2, before we find that Congress lies under the mandated duty of providing for a decennial census. Failure to make such provision would be plainly unconstitutional. Congress is under an affirmative duty to assemble at least once a year. Each House must keep a journal. Congress must provide compensation for its own members, for the President, and for the Article III judges.

The President lies under the highly general affirmative duty to "take Care that the Laws be faithfully executed." Here is exhibited a characteristic that may be seen to inhere to some degree in all the most important duties mandated by the Constitution. The President cannot do everything imaginable to bring it about that the laws be faithfully executed; he is limited by his own physical and mental powers, by other claims on these, and by the amplitude of the means put at his disposal by Congress. The duty has to be a duty to act prudently within these limits, without ulterior motive, sensitive to the force of the powerful conscience-stirring word "faithfully." It cannot be any more—or, I should think, any less—than that. But is it not a duty?

Let us take a closer look at some of the mandated congressional duties. The duty to provide for the mandated decennial census must be a duty to commit reasonable resources, in a prudent way, to producing a serviceably accurate count; to produce a wholly accurate count, as of any given moment, is rigorously impossible, and the fact that the census is mandated to be taken only once in ten years shows that a reasonable approximation is enough to satisfy the needful equality in constituency basis. Yet who can doubt that a congressman who openly refused to vote for any census, or who would vote only for a census-taking procedure which he knew to be grossly flawed, would be in flagitious breach of constitutional duty?

Something like this must be said of Congress' affirmative duty to appropriate money for compensating the President, the judges, and indeed its own members. The words "a compensation" must mean an amount of money that reasonably compensates; otherwise the provision, thrice carefully set out in respect of all the principal officers of the United States, could easily be brought to nothing. Nobody can say, with any show of reason, that there is a duty to compensate the President at one exactly calculable level. Yet a Congress that refused to appropriate a reasonable compensation for the President would be in breach of constitutional duty.

All or most of the constitutional duties expressly set out combine two characteristics. They are, on one hand, real duties. But they can be fulfilled by good-faith action, over a pretty wide and not distinctly bounded range. In these respects they resemble a very great many duties in law outside constitutional law, as well as many duties outside law.

There is then nothing exotic to the Constitution in the

proposition that a constitutional justice of livelihood should be recognized, and should be felt by the President and Congress as laying upon them serious constitutional duty. In the early phases of this work, I find I am most often asked the question, "How much?" or "Where will you draw the line?" (So many people are more anxious about "drawing the line" than about getting food out to hungry children.) I will come back to this later, but I think it well to try to suggest, at the beginning, that the establishment of duty is one thing, while the specification of prudent quantities and means is another—though it must be remembered as well that the decently eligible *range* of means and measures is one thing when you are under no duty at all to act, and quite another when you are under a serious duty to act effectively.

This characteristic continues to be visible as we consider constitutional duties that arise from structural and relational considerations. Congress is literally commanded, as to the support of the other branches of government, only to provide for compensation for the President and the judges. Yet the Constitution assigns to the President duties and functions that require the spending of money—for people, space, travel, supplies, and so on. Since, under Article I, Section 9, clause 7, Congress alone can provide this money, Congress must lie under a constitutional duty to appropriate such money in reasonable amounts, and even to levy taxes, or to borrow, so that the money will be there to appropriate. The same duty is discernible, *mutatis mutandis*, as to the judiciary. These duties, derived from the Constitution, cannot be given arithmetical exactness, but are nonetheless constitutional duties.

That is exactly what I want to see recognized as the duty

of Congress: continually to move, by the general diffusion of welfare, to give life to a constitutional justice of livelihood, and so to prepare the way for the tasks allotted to government in the Declaration of Independence: "to effect their Safety *and* Happiness."

When we are faced with difficulties of "how much," it is often helpful to step back and think small, and to ask not, "What is the whole extent of what we are bound to do?" but rather, "What is the clearest thing we ought to do first?" When we descend to that level, one reasonable answer occurs. Somebody's count has been that a million and a half people in the State of New York are undernourished. About half our black children under six live in poverty, which very commonly entails malnutrition. Some helpless old people have been known to eat dog food when they could get it; it is not recorded that any Cabinet member has yet tried this out on elderly persons in his own extended family. Now you can bog down in a discussion about the exact perimeter of "decent livelihood," or you can cease for a moment from that commonly diversionary tactic and note that, wherever the penumbra may be, malnourished people are not enjoying a decent livelihood. In a constitutional universe admitting serious attention to the Declaration of Independence, a malnourished child is not enjoying a "right to the pursuit of happiness."

And we are very lucky herein, because we know pretty much what to do. We suffered chronic, endemic malnutrition in America. We got rid of it, humanly speaking, by food stamps, school lunches, and a few smaller measures. Then we just let it come back, because we wanted our own taxes lowered. The Great Society nutrition programs, widely spoken

of as having somehow failed, in fact succeeded brilliantly—
a thing that often happens when you attack a problem directly
and simply, giving hungry people more food the shortest way,
instead of feeding them rancid metaphors about boats that rise
when the tide rises. All we have to do is reinstitute adequate
funding for these programs. Then we can think about the next
thing. We won't have to think very long.

I know that I'm talking into the political wind. The country is now infatuated with an idol called "the economy," which
the high priests seem to agree is doing real well, though millions of children are not getting enough to eat, and millions
of adults who want work cannot find it. But winds change;
they always have, and doubtless they always will. A period of
no power is a period for the reformation of thought, to the
end that when power returns it may be more skillfully, more
fittingly, used. The way I want to see thought reformed is by
our ceasing to view the elimination of poverty as a sentimental matter, as a matter of compassion, and our starting to
look on it as a matter of justice, of constitutional right.

Let me say summarily that I know the judicial courts probably cannot handle this matter comprehensively—though
perhaps we may come to know more about that later, through
trial. But Congress too is bound by the Constitution; that instrument imposes many affirmative duties in Congress. Of
course no exhaustive and detailed blueprint of constitutionally required action can be laid out, now or ever, but this fact
is not to be taken to make impossible the discernment of legal
duty, including constitutional duty.

It's hard to know when to stop this argument—or even why
one had to start it. The facts speak: infant mortality, hungry

children, poverty-blighted lives, and the exceedingly plain relation of these and other such things to the pursuit of happiness. The person who needs a lot of argument on this probably won't be convinced by argument. But this chapter, as its title shows, at least aims at shifting the issue, in some minds, from an issue of sentiment, an issue of compassion, to an issue of constitutional justice. This kind of justice must be done, or we will never attain to any other kind of justice. The general diffusion of material welfare is an indispensable part in the general diffusion of the right to the pursuit of happiness.

## Chapter 6

# OF TIME
# AND THE
# CONSTITUTION

    I have always been haunted—both troubled and nourished in spirit—by certain words near the close of the Preamble to our Constitution: ". . . and our Posterity. . . ." These words start up the music of human time—the music of memory, and the vastly open-chorded music of hope. It is in that time—in its fleetingness and in its infinity—that our Constitution has its ordainment and establishment.

    How much time are we talking about, thus far?

I spoke those words to a meeting of a then-new Board of Governors of the American Bar Association, in 1991.

"Time" (in a different sense from the meaning of the legal phrase) "is of the essence" in considering the Constitution, and therefore its system of human rights. The thesis of this book—that our constitutional law of human rights is underdeveloped, unnourished by the three basic commitments that still might be called on to form it—generates questions of time.

1. First, has time made these unredeemed commitments stale? Are we merely stirring the dust of an irrelevant and perhaps not serviceably accessible antiquity?

2. Is it too late, because of abundant and well-reasoned precedent, to effect the change I have advocated here, and so to bring down into modern and future years the epochal commitments of the Declaration of Independence, the life-giving rule of construction of the hitherto virtually unused Ninth Amendment, and the fulfillment of Lincoln's sacred prophecy: that "new birth of freedom" that I think ought to be taken to have been provided for in the "citizenship" and "privileges and immunities" clauses of the first words of the Fourteenth Amendment?

3. As to the future, what kind of development dare we dream of for time to come, if these ideas make their way?

To answer the pervading question I posed myself when addressing the American Bar people—"How much time are we talking about?"—everything depends on the purpose of that general question, and the frame within which it is asked. For purposes of these questions I have just deployed, human life is the right standard of measure. The Protagorean saying, "Man is the measure of all things," is not helpful for intergalactic distances, or for the mass of an electron. But for a history as long or as short as that of the United States Constitution and its laws, it will serve; indeed no other is really imaginable. I cannot, I believe, improve on what I said to the Bar Governors in 1991, just a few days before yesterday:[1]

James Madison was born in 1751; he died in 1836. Benjamin Harrison was born in 1833, and died in 1901; he was thus a child of three when Madison died. Dwight Eisenhower, born in 1890, was eleven when Benjamin Harrison died. Eisenhower died in 1969, 218 years after the birth of Madison. I start with Madison because of his indelible character as chief among the makers of the Constitution. The other two names were suggested by closeness of fit. Altogether, what is shown is that just three human lives, none phenomenally long, can comfortably cover 218 years. Measured backward from now, that count of years takes us back to 1779, three years after the Declaration of Independence, and eight years before the Constitution was sent out from the Philadelphia Convention.

I like to take the reach of my country's time in more personal ways.

Long, long ago, I had a strong friendship with a black man who had been raised to the age of fifteen as a slave. He was freed when the Union troops reached Texas. He had, then, been born about 1850, the year John C. Calhoun died. In Austin there were in my early days Confederate veterans in some number. I used to play with the gold watch one of them carried. Many of the old black people in Austin, when I was, say, ten, had personally been slaves; for that, they needed only to be a little over sixty.

Looking the other way in time, I've been teaching law, these years, to people in their early twenties; I've gotten to know many of them rather well, in quite recent days as well as in the longer past. On any conservative estimate, a good number of these people will live at least sixty years more, some a good deal more—very senior alumni and alumnae of the Yale and Columbia Law Schools, leaders in the mid–twenty-first century.

I won't squeeze these figures, for they can be only approximate; I hope all my students will reach one hundred. But the figures show that one person of my age can have talked about slavery with a man who had been a slave for fifteen years, and then can talk about the American future with young people supremely fitted to face and to shape that future for long into the twenty-first century. My reach in time—through voices I have heard and ears that have heard my voice—is something over two hundred years, not so far from the entire span, up to now, of our nation's life under our Constitution.

Let me take my own mother. She was born in 1885. As a young woman, she saw the first automobiles come to Hillsboro, Texas—though I believe an old buggy remained, until about the time of my own birth, the Hillsboro family's only means of transportation. She died in 1975, two months short of ninety—five or six years after she watched television coverage of the first landing on the moon.

Now people were born in 1816, and some of these lived to the same age my mother attained. As far as time is concerned, one of them, when about sixteen, could have had a talk with the aged James Madison, who remained amenable to conversation until near the very end. This eager young interlocutor would have lived until 1905; before that time my mother, an alert young woman of nearly nineteen, who had taken all the prizes in school, might have listened, eager in her turn, to such a person's reminiscences of that meeting with Madison. Then their talk might have turned to the newfangled automobile.

Time is little understood, hard to measure in the mind. But the obvious calculations I have played with lead me to believe that our feelings about our problems of today, and about the bearing of the past upon these problems, are too much colored by an illusory projection of a very considerable antiquity.

With these measures in mind, let us turn to the first of these questions I have put: Are we so far from the Declaration of Independence, from the Ninth Amendment, from the Fourteenth Amendment that we cannot understand what they are saying?

"Speech community" is a flexible term. I know that I talked with my maternal grandmother with no sense of any difficulty in our understanding one another. I know I would and could have talked with the same ease with my maternal grandfather, had he not died quite early. She was born in about 1860 in Norway, and he in 1857 (the year of the Dred Scott case) in Louisiana. This intimate familial speech community covers an eighty-one-year-old man, and people born about sixty years before he was born. Either of these two grandparents, so far as time goes, could have talked with an old person who in childhood had looked up at the face of George Washington. My grandmother's life and mine, even in their considerable overlap, cover about 155 years, more than all the time from the Fourteenth Amendment to now, and considerably more than half the time back to the Declaration of Independence.

Of course there are slow changes in language, even in such a short period. George Washington would not have understood the word "automobile," just as we do not perhaps understand the word "civility" quite as he did. But the assumption that eighteenth-century language is something like as incomprehensible to our minds as the language of King Alfred, or even of Chaucer, is unbased. We have to ask in each instance what makes us think the language under our eyes was used with important difference in those times.

The terms we have to deal with in our present context are few, and I do think not in the least problematic: the phrase "life, liberty, and the pursuit of happiness" in the Declaration, the rule of construction in the Ninth Amendment, and the "privileges and immunities" formula in the Fourteenth Amendment.

Let us take the naming of the "pursuit of happiness" in the Declaration. This is a thoroughly general phrase. What is it that would make you think that the meaning of these words has changed in their generality? "Happiness" may be a problematic concept, in these days as in those of the Declaration— and in much the same ways then as now. But words are bound by context, and by the nature of life, and it is not "happiness" that is guaranteed, but the right to "pursue," to seek, to try to attain it. In immediate context it stands side by side with the word "liberty." What did the *"pursuit* of happiness," by the exercise of one's "liberty," mean in 1776 that it doesn't now mean?

The Ninth Amendment rule of construction is of at least as obvious a meaning. The designation of the rights that are to be preserved from denial or disparagement, as those *"retained by the people,"* makes just as clear a reference to the rights claimed in the Declaration (some thirteen years earlier) as it can now be seen to make.

The phrase "privileges and immunities," uttered in the Fourteenth Amendment when my maternal grandfather was about eleven, cannot be shown to have suffered any sea-change since at the latest 1825, when, in the leading case on the Article IV "privileges and immunities," Justice Washington explicitly and verbatim included the "right to the pursuit of happiness" as one of them. The only change has been the putting onto the Fourteenth Amendment phrase (in the *Slaughterhouse Cases*) of a jerry-built gloss that deprived it of *all* operational meaning. Whether we can leapfrog over that barrier depends on our assessment of what warrant the Court had for setting it up—a question I have already fully discussed, in Chapter 2 above (I remind you that this gloss was so bizarre that knowledge of it did not become diffused in lexicographic circles—see p. 26 above).

On the whole, to answer the first of my questions, there is just no reason at all for seeing in the passage of time any ground for treating any of these terms as puzzling. It is interesting to note that this is true of most of the expressions in the Constitution and in the statutes contemporary with that document—and later with the Fourteenth Amendment. To confirm this, start reading Article I. You will hit a few terms not now colloquial (like the use of "electors" rather than "voters" in Article I, Section 2), but almost all these tiny difficulties are resolved by the immediate context. In the very example just given, you have no difficulty in understanding who are to be the "voters" who elect the "Congressmen"—also a term that does not occur in the Constitution. The great Document contains some legal terms of art, which are not more than momentarily problematic, some words of indefinite semantic borders, then as now (e.g., "emolument"), a couple of shamed concealments ("other persons" equals "slaves"), and a few imaginable syntactic problems, such as in Article IV, Section 2 (see above, p. 49), but on the whole the Constitution is a piece of language still easily readable as language—though seeing into its deep structure and implications may have been and still may be a much more complicated matter. What I am asserting is that these three prime commitments to human rights are similarly readable by anybody who has a good command of English, and (in case the word "privilege" gives momentary difficulty) a 1939 Unabridged Merriam-Webster dictionary or its equivalent.

It's worth saying, too, that even if we found a letter dated 1788 from Edward Rutledge to Roger Sherman, setting out that Rutledge, in signing the Declaration of Independence, had thought it the general view on that occasion that "the pursuit of happiness" meant only the "pursuit of material prosperity," such a letter could scarcely be looked on as an authority; it is only one cup of water scooped out of the vast ocean of eighteenth-century English. It is my very strong view that we ought to make what we can out of the language *chosen by authority to be the language of authority,* and resort to other language, which is all we can possibly have, only when the authoritative language is of real obscurity. None of the language in our three principal commitments to human rights comes close to such obscurity—except possibly the word "privilege," which we can look up in the Merriam-Webster, where we find it to be highly multivocal, but with one meaning right on the money (see above, p. 26).

I have labored this point pretty hard. That is because I have discovered how prevalent the practice is of turning at once to general considerations and to scraps of collateral discourse, while never giving the chosen authoritative language itself a chance. I have more than once been in an argument about the lawfulness of judicial review of state laws, for their conformity to the national Constitution, with people who turned out never to have read Article VI of the Constitution, or, if they had read it, showed no sign of remembering it. If you read it for yourself you'll see that it completely settles the question whether judges *in their courts* are duty-bound to treat the national Constitution as a superior law to any state law, and to decide the cases before them accordingly.

I could multiply such instances. There is very serious truth underlying the (quite apocryphal) story that a celebrated Supreme Court Justice once remarked, in a case concerning the meaning of an Act of Congress, "There is no legislative history available on this point, so we shall have to look at the text of the statute."

But let me not dwell on this any more, lest I convey the impression that I know of some unofficial, unauthoritative "history" of such weight as mortally to impeach what I think is the clear meaning of our three commitments to human rights. I do not know of any such material, and I believe if it were at all strong I would by this time have heard of it. But, as I formerly wrote in this general context, "Those who believe in astrology always know more about astrology than do those who do not believe in astrology."

The second question I have asked is whether it's too late to effect the change I am advocating.

This is just a question we are asking about ourselves, about our political society. It is obviously not too late, if we are in sufficient numbers resolved that it not be too late.

But while this remains true, the question can be made a little more malleable by asking two sub-questions. First, has so much authority, very high and carefully considered authority, accrued around the rejection of the force in law of these three great commitments that it becomes too hard to fight against that authority? Secondly, how characteristic is it of our constitutional law system that it can change its direction, even after a long time?

As to the accrual of authority, it will be helpful to take up each of these three prime commitments one by one.

The Declaration of Independence was appealed to in some very early cases, though not, I think, in the Supreme Court. These cases would not in themselves suffice to establish a consensus that the Declaration could not play a part in law. Neither do they establish the contrary. As to this, I think we cannot pass over the fact that the Declaration became a rallying-point for anti-slavery forces, and was an embarrassment to the pro-slavery people. It was inextricably caught up in the most terrible of American questions—the question that woke Jefferson like a firebell in the night, and that at last caused our great Civil War. That judges should treat it gingerly is more than understandable—such diffidence was something like inevitable. The best we can say is that no Supreme Court ever rejected in terms the idea that the Declaration was a primary source of legal right. The 1825 *Corfield* case, discussed above (see pp. 49–50), goes a long way toward upholding the authority of the Declaration in establishing the principal human rights protected in law, and the authority of that case, though in a perverse way, was recognized in the *Slaughterhouse Cases* opinion.

The same is true (and I am not historian enough to think I fully know why) of the Ninth Amendment, whether considered as a thing in itself or as an entitlement of the entry of the Declaration into constitutional law. I would conjecture—and no more than that, for I have no right—that the Ninth Amendment lay sleeping because it too might open up a path for additional rights antagonistic to slavery. Certainly it would have done so if connected to the Declaration. There was an anti-slavery thesis, floated by how many people I don't know, that the national government was barred by the Fifth Amendment from giving any affirmative aid to slavery, such as the drastic Fugitive Slave law of 1850. Perhaps it was feared that the creative freedom seemingly promised by the Ninth Amendment might give rise to other anti-slavery contentions not textually originating in Amendment V or other Bill of Rights provisions. Or perhaps there was heard by others than Jefferson the clang of a firebell in the night.

Finally (and most paradoxically!) we come to the *Slaughterhouse Cases*, wherein the third of our great commitments was dirked. That case is all the top authority we have against us.

I have written the immediately foregoing paragraphs with great diffidence, because I control neither the broad historical source-material nor the instructed concepts needful to explain why it was that the early record of the Declaration and the Ninth Amendment was so dreary. I strongly feel that it had to do with slavery. I even think it probable that the *Slaughterhouse* Court, realizing that giving full scope to a set of "privileges and immunities of citizens of the United States," which now definitely included blacks, would open a wide door for claims of right by the freedmen, paled at what it saw as the unmanageableness of this. In a country founded largely on slavery, a country wherein slavery continued for nearly ninety years after it was proclaimed that all men were "created equal," with the God-given right to liberty, a country wherein (after the great War and the abolition of chattel slavery) every sleazy trick concoctable was brought into play, and blessed by the Court, to keep black people in their place—in such a country, I think it not really far-fetched to suspect strong subjacent connections between anti-black racism and many puzzling judicial or political actions or inactions. Certainly the underdevelopment of a system of human rights, the election not to make very much of our three great commitments to comprehensive human rights, is not really astounding, just as it is no great breach of probability to guess that the failure of the United States now to go to a civilized system of general medical care results, in part at least, from a reluctance to give that much to poor black people.

The upshot is that, while there is little venerable authority availing of the Declaration and the Ninth Amendment, there is no daunting authority against their use. The problem-case is of course *Slaughterhouse*, but that case is not even a good piece of legal shoddy, fit to stuff mattresses.

Now, granting that the strong affirmative use of the great commitments on which I rely has not occurred up to now, is that enough to discourage you? How characteristic is it of our constitutional legal system to change its direction?

In 1842, the Supreme Court, in *Swift v. Tyson*,[2] held that the federal courts, hearing cases involving issues of state common (that is to say, non-statutory) law, were to apply their own version of this common law, rather than the version the relevant State followed in its own courts.

In 1938, in *Erie R.R. v. Tompkins*,[3] after nearly one hundred years and hundreds of cases in which the rule of *Swift v. Tyson* had been distinctly followed and applied, the Supreme Court overruled *Swift v. Tyson*.

In 1922, the Supreme Court said in *Prudential Insurance Co. v. Cheek*:

> But, as we have stated, neither the Fourteenth Amendment nor any other provision of the Constitution of the United States imposes upon the States any restrictions about "freedom of speech" or the "liberty of silence"; nor, we may add, does it confer any right of privacy upon either persons or corporations.[4]

When those words were uttered in the opinion of the Court, the Fourteenth Amendment had been around for fifty-four years—"substantive due process" had already strongly come on the scene.

By 1937, just fifteen years after *Cheek*, Mr. Justice Cardozo, in the famous *Palko* passage I have quoted (see above pp. 94–95), was explaining, after the fact, why it was that the free-speech guaranty of the First Amendment was held binding on the States. For it was in 1937—only fifteen years after *Cheek*—that the Supreme Court for the first time reversed a state court conviction on substantive free-speech grounds.[5] In the sixty years since, it has been almost forgotten that the Supreme Court said what it did in *Prudential Insurance Co. v. Cheek*. It just doesn't fit in.

In 1867, the Supreme Court first decided a case *in favor* of a person who claimed that a State's action impermissibly "burdened inter-state commerce."[6] (The doctrine relied on had been spoken of with qualified approval, in principle, in

1851[7]—but even that is sixty-four years after the adoption of the Constitution.)

In 1949, in *Hood & Sons v. Du Mond,*[8] Mr. Justice Jackson, for the Court, wrote:

> The Commerce Clause is one of the most prolific sources of national power and an equally prolific source of conflict with legislation of the states. While the Constitution vests in Congress the power to regulate commerce among the states, it does not say what the states may or may not do in the absence of congressional action. . . . Perhaps even more than by interpretation of its written words, this Court has advanced the solidarity and prosperity of this Nation by the meaning it has given to these great silences of the Constitution. . . . [The] principle that our economic unit is the Nation, which alone has the gamut of powers necessary to control the economy, including the vital power of erecting customs barriers against foreign competition, has as its corollary that the states are not separable economic units.

Never has the absence of a constitutional text supporting a line of constitutional decisions (a very common thing) been dealt with more elegantly than in the phrase "these great silences of the Constitution"! Still, the decisions are there, issuing in steady progression from "the great silence."

Since 1871, before and after 1949, formulation has succeeded metaphysical formulation, line after tormented line has been drawn, to mark out the areas of permissible and impermissible state interference with interstate commerce—as to migration, as to mudguards, as to milk, as to minnows. This regime, which the Court in *Hood* sees as so important to national economic unity, and which takes up a lot of space in modern constitutional-law casebooks, is virtually a post–Civil War creation.

There is an even more profound point to be made here. If a "great silence" is all that is needed to generate this mass of decisions—striking down, year after year, laws of the States, and thus frustrating the state "majorities" that made them— why should it be disturbing if the same thing should occur, with equal prolificity of doctrine, in regard to human rights? As it is, there isn't even a "great silence" here; we have the three texts I have been exploring. In the passage I have just quoted from Mr. Justice Jackson, he said, "[The] principle that our economic unit is the Nation . . . has as its corollary that the states are not separable economic units." When we at last face up to the Declaration of Independence, can we think that it generates no "corollary" that the States are not to be separable moral units, with respect to their "securing human rights"?

Then interference by the States with the practical enjoyment of the national "privileges and immunities" is an interference with values that the national government was established to maintain and is obligated to maintain—to "secure." It is state interference with the effective working of a comprehensive national plan of human rights. Even if the national bestowal of *state* citizenship were thought not to import a command that the human rights of the designated persons be binding directly on the States, the States would nevertheless be forbidden to frustrate, to bring to nothing, the obligation and therefore the *function* of the national government in regard to human rights, or to the values the national plan aims at advancing. The symmetry with the "economic nationhood" cases is striking.

It is in the implications of this symmetry that understanding of the high political place of general national protection of human rights, against the States, is to be found. The "economic nationhood" cases rest not on any particular words of the Constitution, but rather on a general concept of our national "union." Can there not also be made out a legitimate and authenticated concept of the nation, the "union," as one *wherein* human rights are to *prevail?* To deny this is total denial of the authority of the Declaration of Independence, even as a statement of the nation's goals and reason for being. Why would we do that, while at the same time finding in the "great silences" of the Constitution a concept of *economic* nationhood, capable of generating innumerable judicial decisions? What would support this choice of free trade over the claim of the American people to enjoy, as a whole people, the benefits of living under a unified regime of human rights? This would be inexplicably perverse, particularly since we do not have to choose between these concepts of nationhood, but can live by both of them. Indeed, they overlap in a penumbra between them, as in the right-to-travel cases. But can a nation live by trade alone?

Can we really bear to say, even (and above all) to ourselves, that the unity of this Union is a unity only in governmental power and in economic exchange, but is not a moral unity in the observance of human rights? Even the Preamble of the Constitution strongly speaks against this: "to . . . secure the Blessings of Liberty to ourselves and our Posterity." We betray this very statement of purpose, uttered at the creation of the national government, if we accept and act upon the view that there is no national law of general human rights binding on the States.

These structural considerations lead to the same conclusion as the texts: "Our Federalism" need not be, must not be, the "Catch-22" of human rights—the fine-print "catch" that fatally undermines the boldface guarantee.

In 1791, the Sixth Amendment guaranteed the accused person in criminal proceedings the right "to have the assistance of counsel for his defense." In *Johnson v. Zerbst* (1938),[9] the Supreme Court first held that this was an absolute Constitutional right *in the Federal courts*, and that assigned counsel must be provided. There had been differences in practice in the federal courts, but (*148 years* after the adoption of the Sixth Amendment) the Supreme Court held the right to be an absolute one for all federal criminal defendants.

Meanwhile, in 1930, the Supreme Court held that the Fourteenth Amendment "due process" clause required the appointment of counsel in state *capital* cases, where the defendants were indigent and ignorant.[10] Thirty-two years later, and a total of nearly one hundred years after the passage of the Fourteenth Amendment, in *Gideon v. Wainwright* the Supreme Court *first held* that counsel must be furnished in all serious state criminal cases.[11]

Now I could go on and on with this. Consider carefully the elapsed times—it took sixty-two years after the passage of the Fourteenth Amendment for the Court to hold, even in a state case involving eight death sentences, that "due process" required the appointment of counsel for indigent state defendants! It took nearly a hundred years (after much backing and forthing) for the Court to decide that counsel must be furnished in *all* serious state criminal cases.

On the other hand, the Court can reverse itself fairly quickly. There elapsed fifteen years between its 1922 *Prudential* statement that there was no free speech as against the States, and the holding (soon greatly proliferated) that such protection did exist.

Now in the matters covered in this book, we are dealing with something that, if it is a mistake, was one of the biggest mistakes, doubtless the very biggest, in our history—the failure to make any use, in law, of our unique and irreplaceable national heritage of committed principles.

On the other hand, as to the Declaration and the Ninth Amendment, there is not even any impressive decisional authority to "overrule." The overruling of *Slaughterhouse* ought to occur, but even that is not seriously out of the time-scale I have set before you. *Slaughterhouse* came down just a decade before my father was born. It has encouraged no "reliance" of a desirable kind. Indeed, the correction of such a huge mistake could really never be "too late."

I put it to you that there is nothing in the history of these great utterances in our charter of human rights, or in our dealings with hugely consequential precedents, to make us hesitate to move toward the righting of this hugely consequential mistake—the failure to use these precious utterances, "in their spirit and in their entirety."

How would such a resolve come about? How would it work out in the future?

One can safely say: "Very slowly."

The first step would be the formation of a new professional and public opinion around the idea that we have gone astray in rejecting, perhaps in rather silently repudiating, the mighty force of these commitments (the Declaration, the Ninth Amendment, and the citizenship and privileges and immunities clauses of the Fourteenth Amendment) as the ultimate complex source of our commitment to an open-ended, open-textured system of human rights in general. This book is obviously an attempt to push that process along. If such a movement of professional and public opinion does at last go forward, nobody will ever know what "caused" it; it will be the result of the efforts of many, many people.

When we turn to the chief and most easily invocable holders of power over the subject, our Supreme Court, we can expect nothing very dramatic, no definite "event." You have sampled, just above, illustrations of the slowness with which our judiciary moves toward change, toward the ultimate acceptance of the obvious—such as the obvious truth that no defendant can have a reliable expectation of getting "due process of law" if he has no right to a lawyer. It took fifty-eight years for the Court to accept and act on the obvious truth that segregation by law is pervadingly an insult to black people, an "assertion of their inferiority," and is massively harmful to them in more concrete ways.

But these cases, like some of the other examples I have given you of judicial glaciality, involved relatively simple issues. A dramatic event, like the *Brown* case, was clear in outline, though far from free of subsidiary problems of implementation.

By contrast, what I am advocating in this book is a change in method, in total outlook, in perception of the very foundations of our human-rights law. If it comes, my own thought is that it will come as a *realization* not only of the power of our cardinal commitments to human rights, but even a realization that all along, particularly in this century, we have lamely and inarticulately decided a miscellany of cases that can confidently be justified only on the grounds of our three *general* commitments:

> People have a right to practice contraception.[12]
>
> Persons have a right to marry, even people who cannot prove that the children of a prior marriage will not become public charges.[13]
>
> A grandmother has a right to bring her own grandchildren to live with her.[14]
>
> People have a right to send their children to a religious or military school,[15] or if their religion so commands, to send them to no high school at all.[16]
>
> There is a general law of free speech and of freedom of religion *applicable to the States*, though the First Amendment, in its terms, applies only to the national *Congress*. (As to this enormous body of federal constitutional restriction on the States, see Cardozo's justification in the *Palko* case, and my critique of that justification, above pp. 93–97)
>
> A prisoner has a constitutional right not to be sterilized for having three felony convictions.[17]
>
> A person has a right to teach and learn a foreign language.[18]
>
> A person has a right to travel from one State to another, without being taxed for doing so.[19]

A female naval lieutenant has a right to have her hus-
band's medical expenses covered, as those of the wife
of a male lieutenant would be—though the equal protection clause of the Fourteenth Amendment does
not, as a matter of text, apply against the national government.[20]

The cases in this miscellany (and it could be augmented)
rest on different constitutional grounds. Most of them either
invoke or seem silently to rely on "substantive due process."
Some seem to have sidestepped reference to any constitutional formula, and proceed directly to invoke the very solem-
nity and importance of the right sustained, without bothering
to link it up with any specific textual material. The explanation of the right to travel from one State to another has been
explained in a number of ways, so many and varied that in *U.S.
v. Guest*[21] Justice Stewart says that it doesn't matter what the
correct explanation is, because "all agree" that the right exists; he later adds, in a footnote, that this right is "in the Constitution," without saying just where.

Our constitutional law has never been wholly "textual."
But these miscellaneous recent cases on human rights seem to
me to evidence, as to human rights, an uneasiness, a discom-
fort, with the conventional (though erroneous) dogma that
human-rights protections must be found in specific texts.
With Stewart's treatment of the right to travel from State to
State (see the last paragraph), compare his dissent in the con-
traceptive case, *Griswold v. Connecticut*,[22] where he says he has
looked at the Constitution and could "find nothing" in it that
invalidated a state law making contraception a crime. And in

turn compare the ease with which the same justice accepted
the derivation of a general substantive maritime law from a
mere grant of *judicial jurisdiction* in admiralty cases to the federal courts.[23]

There's something out of joint here, some major disloca-
tion of method.

Now look over the cases I have just listed, above. *Would not
each and all of them* fit comfortably into the explanatory cate-
gory of "the right to the pursuit of happiness"?

Is not the prohibition of contraception a deadly blow at the
pursuit of happiness, forcing on couples the alternative of ab-
staining from intercourse, or having children they do not
now, perhaps for very good reason, want to have, or think it
right to have?

Is not the denial of the freedom to "exercise" one's religion
a cold obstruction to the "pursuit of happiness," in the very
way that countless millions have tried to pursue it?

Jefferson said "knowledge is happiness." Is not interference
with freedom of communication an efficacious way of chok-
ing off this kind of the "pursuit of happiness"?

Are not a grandmother and her orphan grandchildren
barred from one kind of the "pursuit of happiness," when they
are told they may not live together in her house?

Are not parents who are forbidden by law to send their
child to a military school being balked in the pursuit of that
high happiness that comes when you think you are doing the
best thing for your child?

Let me put it another way: In the "substantive due process"
discourse, extended as it is, the phrase *"fundamental values"* plays
a big part. But how do you proceed even to a first approxi-

mation to knowing what values are "fundamental"? Are they
not the "values" of the Declaration, the values that people pursue in their pursuit of happiness?

What I am suggesting to you is that the frank acceptance
of the "right to the pursuit of happiness" as a prime—probably *the* prime—foundation for a law of human rights would
have a refreshing, clarifying effect on the feeling of legitimacy
in most—if not all—constitutional human-rights material: It
would easily explain most of the cases as to which difficulty
has been felt.

It would do more than that. Just to take one random sam-
ple, it would make an open-and-shut case of the claim that
the right to listen to music of your choice and to produce
music of your choice are constitutionally protected. How
could anybody conclude that producing and listening to
music is not an indispensable, a very precious part, of "the pursuit of happiness"? You could skip all that part about how
music resembles speech in some ways but not in others, and
about the question whether "freedom of speech" includes
"freedom to listen," and "freedom not to speak," and go right
to the heart of the matter. Nietzsche said that "life without
music would be a mistake"; some people feel that way, others
are less intense. To some, of course, music is just a bore; they
can "pursue happiness" in their own way. Bless us all!

This kind of simple insight could bring the "right to the
pursuit of happiness" as a touchstone to any human activity
or concern. It would reach out to every field of human rights.
It would make plain the wrong in every kind of discrimination hurtful to women. It goes to the essence of the wrongs
done by the law and outside the law to those having homo-

sexual preferences. It could clarify the ultimate grounds of the banning of racial discrimination against blacks and other racial minorities. I won't try to go through all the other applications; they are as wide as human pursuit of happiness, to which our Declaration is not embarrassed to refer.

This most important factor that would be certain to make the application of, say, the "pursuit of happiness" criterion a slow, and indeed never finished, process is the ongoing assessment, over the range of law and life, of *justification* for governmental activity.

I am not on the enterprise here of searching the largely unknowable psychic content of eighteenth-century people. The matter is much simpler than that. Anybody, in the eighteenth century or the twentieth, who anticipated that a solemn guarantee, like this of the "right to the pursuit of happiness," was an "absolute"—that this "pursuit" was guaranteed to be absolutely immune from the interposition of any obstacles— would be certifiably insane. This plain fact has been clouded, sometimes, by the insistence (now, I believe, shelved under the impact of the facts) that the "freedom of speech" and "free exercise of religion" are "absolute." That view is one that can be held only by somebody who hasn't thought about a sound truck turning up at midnight and bawling obscene curses near a sleeper's window, or a radio broadcast that promises that a mixture of witch hazel and thrice-distilled water will cure skin cancer, or a fundamentalist snake-worshipper driving a herd of rattlesnakes down a street. The interesting and encouraging thing for us is that *although* free speech and freedom of religious exercise are *not* "absolutes," but must over a wide and never quite predictable range yield to suitable justification, these freedoms are very serious constitutional values, having ponderous weight in law, and that justification must, to be of avail, take into account the weight and seriousness of the constitutional commitment, given its source. If this course is followed—and it usually is—in law, then the free speech and freedom of religion guarantees are a part of law, and have real meaning as law.

I am sure that that is all we can ask for the Declaration's "right to the pursuit of happiness," carried down into and through the Ninth and Fourteenth Amendments. What I am asking is that that right be accepted as a pervading part of law, be accorded in law the great weight given by the authority of the Declaration and its sequels, and that, in view of that authority, all claims of justification should have to be judged, if they are to prevail, on a scale suitable for allowing such justification.

That is all we have now as to free speech, which, under this rule, has worked its way into the whole legal fabric, and plays a vital, serious part therein.

We do not have this now as to "the pursuit of happiness." If later on we do, the result will be a thoroughgoing and never-ending working-over of the regime of law, with attention to the enormous weight of the principle, given its origin.

## An Afterword

"Now he belongs to the ages."

These words of Stanton, on his learning that Lincoln had died, assure us that we are not done with Lincoln. He belongs to our ages, gone and to come. His is the spirit I have invoked to quicken this book.

In one of his best-remembered sayings, he hopefully foretold that "this nation, under God, shall enjoy a new birth of freedom." Lincoln did not use such words lightly.

The distinct event after his death that seemed to announce this "new birth of freedom" was the opening passage of the Fourteenth Amendment, recognizing, as clearly and as broadly as words could do, the "privileges and immunities of the citizens of the United States." These "privileges and immunities" are set out, with becoming breadth, in the Declaration of Independence, the lode-star of Lincoln's life.

Eight years after Lincoln died, our Supreme Court, in the *Slaughterhouse Cases*, did its best to bring to nothing his sacred prophecy. The country has accepted, for a time, that terrible deed.

But the spirit and mind of Lincoln belong to the ages, out of the power of any Court, or of one short period of history, to bring them to nothing. When we are ready, we can take up the work to which he continues to beckon us. If we do so, we will be treading the ways of his journey, from his reverence for the Declaration of Independence to his vision at Gettysburg.

When you will, you can join the supreme company of his great soul.

# Notes

---

CHAPTER 1

[1] *On Reading and Using the Ninth Amendment,* in *Power and Policy in Quest of Law: Essays in Honor of Eugene Rostow* 187 (M. McDougal & W.M. Reisman, eds. [Norwell, MA: Kluwer Academic Publishers, 1984]), reprinted in C. Black, *The Humane Imagination* 186 (Woodbridge, CT: Ox Bow Press, 1987) and in *The Rights Retained by the People* 337 (R. Barnett, ed. [Lanham, MD: University Press of America, 1989]); *Further Reflections on the Constitutional Justice of Livelihood,* 86 *Columbia Law Review* 1103, 1104 (1986); *"One Nation Indivisible": Unnamed Human Rights Against the States,* 65 *St. John's Law Review* 17 (1991).

[2] In this connection, consider with special care the points on p. 37, below.

[3] See Black, *On Reading and Using the Ninth Amendment,* Chapter 1, footnote 1.

[4] See especially Section 25 of the Judiciary Act of 1789, quoted and discussed below at pp. 120–121.

[5] Usually of a negative and constricting kind, often exploiting, perhaps unconsciously, the inbuilt ambiguity and even

multivocality of the phrase "did not intend," and whistling past the evident *generality* of the language under interpretation.

[6]*Tinker v. Des Moines School District*, 393 U.S. Reports 503 (1969). Of course, the analogic and functional extension of the freedoms of "speech" and "press" is far wider than a single example can do more than hint at.

[7]*U.S. v. Causby*, 328 U.S. 256 (1946).

[8]*Citizens Against Rent Control v. Berkeley*, 454 U.S. 290 (1981).

[9]See my *Structure and Relationship in Constitutional Law (Baton Rouge: Louisiana State University Press, 1969)*, passim.

[10]*Crandall v. Nevada*, 73 U.S. 35 (1867).

[11]*Corfield v. Coryell*, 4 Wash. CC. 371, 6 F. Cas. 546 (C.C.E.D Pa 1825). The most important passage in this opinion is quoted on pp. 49–50 below.

[12]16 Wallace (88 U.S.) 36 (1873).

## CHAPTER 2

[1]Black, *The American Law of Free Speech as Applied Against the States*, in *Faculty Presentations, Moscow Conference on Law and Economic Cooperation* 177 (1990). Paper presented to panel in Moscow on "Glasnost."

[2]*Corfield v. Coryell*, cited above, Chapter 1, footnote 11.

[3]17 U.S. 316 (1819).

[4]The *Slaughterhouse Cases*, 83 U.S. 36 (1871).

[5]*Havenstein v. Lynham*, 100 U.S. 483 (1880).

[6]*Oregon v. U.S.*, 366 U.S. 643 (1961).

[7]I will be back at you once more (pp. 80–84) with a sum-up of the exceedingly profound relations of the anti-nationalist doctrines of Calhoun to the holding in *Slaughterhouse*.

[8]See above pp. 49–50. You should reread this much-quoted passage with care at this time.

[9]*Butler v. Boston & Savannah S.S. Co.*, 130 & S. 527 (1889); *Kermarec v. Cie Gen. Transatlantique*, 358 U.S. 625 (1959).

[10]I am reminded here of a story told me by the late Allison Dunham, who for a few years, some forty years ago, occupied an office next to mine at Columbia Law School. He was stopped for speeding by an officer in Pennsylvania. Taken immediately before a Justice of the Peace, he was fined some $10. Fresh from his clerkship with Mr. Justice Stone, and recalling a recent Supreme Court case, he said, "Your Honor, may I respectfully inquire whether a part of this fine will go to you personally?" "Yes," the J.P. answered. "In that case," replied Dunham, "the recent case of *Toomey v. Ohio* says that you may not judge this case." "Wait a minute," answered the "judge." "What court was that case decided by?" Dunham played his trump: "Your Honor, by the Supreme Court of the United States!" "Well," said the "judge," "that's all right. This is Pennsylvania." I think Dunham paid the fine.

[11]It is a venerable hypothesis that the strange disappearance of the Fourteenth Amendment "privileges and immunities" clause from the toolkit of working law is to be explained by a reluctance in the Court to exclude aliens from benefits that the clause might otherwise have been held to engender. I find this ridiculous, in regard to a century covering the infamous Chinese Exclusion Case, *Chae Chan Ping v. United States*, 130 U.S. 581 (1889), the somewhat later cases that denied anything like even procedural due process to persons of oriental appearance who were so much as *alleged* not to be citizens, and the deplorable anti-alien cases of even later

decades. But in any event, the fear of harm to aliens is easily exorcised.

In *Truax v. Raich,* 239 U.S. 33 (1915), the Court indicated that Congress' decision to admit certain aliens was tantamount to a direction that they be allowed by the States to live amongst us and to enjoy in a substantial sense the privileges conferred by this admission. (The *Truax* Court, perhaps redundantly but very significantly, held that aliens' admission brought them under the "equal protection" clause, as to discriminations between them and citizens.) The Court has flip-flopped on the detailed application of this principle, but the principle is evidently sound, and serviceable as a complete answer to the fear, doubtless in many cases a pretended fear, that it would be dangerous to give much scope to the "privileges and immunities" clause, because the benefits extended thereby to citizens could not be thought to be within the reach of aliens. For a somewhat fuller discussion of the *Truax v. Raich* principle, and its few legitimate qualifications (as to voting and eligibility for major policy-forming public office), see C. Black, *Decision According to Law* 56–62 (New York: W. W. Norton, 1981).

[12]See my *On Worrying About the Constitution,* 55 *University of Colorado Law Review* 469 (1984), reprinted in Black, *The Humane Imagination* 118 (1986).

CHAPTER 3

[1]166 U.S. 226 (1897).

[2]32 U.S. 243 (1833).

[3]198 U.S. 45 (1905).

[4]See Chapter 1 at notes 5 and 7.

[5]*New York Times v. Sullivan,* 376 U.S. 254 (1964).

[6]*Sherbert v. Wiener,* 374 U.S. 398 (1963).

[7]*Edwards v. Aguillard,* 482 U.S. 578 (1987). (The "religion" cases, both as to "establishment" and "free exercise," are confusing and decision oscillates.)

[8]*Meyer v. Nebraska,* 262 U.S. 390 (1923).

[9]*Pierce v. Society of Sisters,* 268 U.S. 510 (1925).

[10]*Griswold v. Connecticut,* 381 U.S. 479 (1965).

[11]*Zablocki v. Redhail,* 434 U.S. 374 (1978).

[12]302 U.S. 319 (1937).

[13]*De Jonge v. Oregon,* 353 (1937).

[14]*Benton v. Maryland,* 395 U.S. 784.

[15]See my *Capital Punishment: The Inevitability of Caprice and Mistake* (New York: W. W. Norton, 2d ed., 1980), Chapter 9, pp. 85–93.

[16]367 U.S. 497 (1961).

[17]381 U.S. 479 (1965).

[18]*Moore v. East Cleveland,* 431 U.S. 494 (1977).

CHAPTER 4

[1]*Griswold v. Connecticut,* cited above, Chapter 3, footnote 10.

[2]Black, *National Lawmaking By Initiative? Let's Think Twice,* in *Human Rights,* Fall 1979, at 28; reprinted in Black, *The Humane Imagination* 66 (1986).

[3]I would like to think that John Marshall had something like this in mind when he strongly spoke in favor of judicial review, in the Virginia ratifying convention: *"To what quarter will you look for protection from an infringement on the constitution, if you will not give the power to the judiciary? There is no other body that can afford such a protection."* (Emphasis added.)

[4]1 Annals of Congress 457 (1789).

## CHAPTER 6

[1]The entire address was later published as "And Our Posterity . . . ," 102 *Yale Law Journal* 1527 (1993). I borrow from it freely here, but with some omissions and changes.

[2]41 U.S. 1 (1842).

[3]304 U.S. 64 (1938).

[4]*Prudential Insurance Co. v. Cheek*, 259 U.S. 530 (1922).

[5]*De Jonge v. Oregon*, 299 U.S. 353.

[6]*Steamship Co. v. Portwardens*, 73 U.S. 31 (1867).

[7]*Cooley v. Board of Wardens*, 53 U.S. 299 (1851).

[8]*H.P. Hood & Sons v. Du Mond*, 336 U.S. 525 (1949).

[9]304 U.S. 458 (1938).

[10]*Powell v. Alabama* 287 U.S. 45 (1932).

[11]370 U.S. 335 (1963).

[12]*Griswold v. Connecticut*, cited above, Chapter 3, footnote 10.

[13]*Zablocki v. Redhail*, cited above, Chapter 3, footnote 11.

[14]*Moore v. East Cleveland*, cited above, Chapter 3, footnote 18.

[15]*Pierce v. Society of Sisters*, cited above, Chapter 3, footnote 9.

[16]*Wisconsin v. Yoder*, 406 U.S. 205 (1972)

[17]*Skinner v. Oklahoma*, 316 U.S. 535 (1942)

[18]*Meyer v. Nebraska*, cited above, Chapter 3, footnote 8.

[19]*Crandell v. Nevada*, cited above, Chapter 1, footnote 10.

[20]*Frontiero v. Richardson*, 411 U.S. 677 (1973)

[21]383 U.S. 745 (1966)

[22]*Griswold v. Connecticut*, cited above, Chapter 3, footnote 10.

[23]See the *Kermarec Case*, cited above, Chapter 2, footnote 9.

## FOREWORD

[1]As for example in Magna Carta or the French Declaration of the Rights of Man.

[2]As described by Thomas Hobbes and Jean Bodin, among others.

[3]The Lawfulness of the Segregation Decisions, 69 Yale L.J. 421 (1960).

[4]Philip Bobbitt, *Constitutional Interpretation* (Blackwell, 1991).

[5]These six modalities are: *historical* (relying on the intentions of the framers and ratifiers of the Constitution); *textual* (looking to the meaning of the words of the Constitution alone, as they would be applied by the average contemporary "man on the street" today; *structural* (inferring rules from the relationships that the Constitution mandates among the structures it sets up); *doctrinal* (applying rules generated by precedent); *ethical* (deriving rules from the commitments that reflect the American ethos of limited government); and *prudential* (seeking to balance the cost and benefits of a particular rule. Ibid.

[6]I was recently accosted by a lawyer on the street—a former government official, I think—who asked me if I thought a sitting president could be indicted. When I said I doubted this, he demanded to know "where in the Constitution it says 'the President is above the law.'" I suppose we saw the same sort of thing at the time of Watergate.